PRAISE FOR
FROM POVERTY TO PROSPERITY

I have three words about this book: Insightful! Spiritual and practical!

*— **Reverend Jim Holley,** PhD*
Pastor Emeritus of the Historic Little Rock Baptist
Church, Detroit, MI

. . .

As colonel of the Michigan State Police (MSP) from 2011 to 2019, I had the pleasure to meet and work closely with Bishop Ira Combs. I found him to be not only a man of great intellect, but his willingness to help support and train the men and women of law enforcement within the MSP was remarkable.

I would often draw wisdom from him on topics of community engagement, statewide political perspectives, civil rights challenges, and key efforts to help bridge equality gaps.

When I retired from the Michigan State Police, after thirty-two years of service, I knew that Bishop Combs had left an everlasting impact on not only me personally but on the leadership within the ranks of a statewide police agency.

To this day I regard him as a trusted friend, mentor, and a man of great faith. I'm confident his book *From Poverty to Prosperity: Work Hard, Work Smart, Figure it Out* will be not only educational but a vivid account of a great man's life.

*— **Colonel Kriste Kibbey Etue** (Retired)*
Michigan State Police

. . .

Bishop Combs gives of himself unselfishly and allows God to use him and bless him. To God be the glory for the things that he has done and is doing through Bishop Combs.

— **Naomi Sessley,** *Evangelist*

. . .

Reverend Combs takes the reader on a fast–paced journey of his life and faith. He highlights pivotal moments where others provided wisdom and guidance that shaped his leadership, his ministry, politics, and faith.

— *Jim Haveman*
Former Director of the Michigan Department
of Community Health

. . .

Endorsing the literary works of a proven apostolic giant whose life is a living epistle and the manifestation of God's promises in His word is an honor and a privilege.

— **Olivia C. Burkett,** *PhD*
Professor of Psychology, William Carey University

. . .

Ira learned from an early age many lessons of hard work, sacrifice, and perseverance. He was blessed to have a principled father who modeled him into the man he became. Having the sense to know when to remove yourself from bad environments was the turning point in Ira's young life. "Truly a blessing from God, because God makes no failures," as Ira recounts, is a strong takeaway from this book. Ira takes great life lessons and strength from the Almighty that inspires the reader.

— *Jennifer S. Carroll*
Former Lieutenant Governor, Florida

. . .

A story of Americana: rising above personal circumstance to inspire faith in others, improve communities, and serve our country.

— ***Sam Willcoxon***
Former CEO, Fidelis SeniorCare

. . .

Bishop Combs's personal reflections on his upbringing, education, and personal and professional experiences provide wonderful insight into the profound ways God desires to use—and can use—faithful and committed people to accomplish His will. Dr. Combs's story inspires readers to submit the entirety of their lives and will to the living God and then watch in amazement as God brings fruitfulness across the entire spectrum of their lives.

— ***Dr. Brent Ellis***
President, Spring Arbor University

. . .

I have known Bishop Combs for many years, going back to when I was a state senator for almost a decade in the nineties. He has always worked tirelessly to make our community and country a better place. His personal path inspires others to follow. I am proud to call him a friend.

— ***Sheriff Michael Bouchard***
Oakland County, Michigan

. . .

Ira Combs shares an American story of faith, family, and grit. His inspirational book details the road to success in its fullest meaning: helping others, building community, and extending hands of friendship. After reading *From Poverty to Prosperity: Work Hard, Work Smart, Figure it Out* you will be encouraged about

America's future. Ira Combs's life is an aspirational story about a compelling American journey.

*— **Bill Schuette***
Former Michigan Attorney General

...

I have known Bishop Ira Combs for more than twenty years. He is a man of principle and integrity. He is wise and generous. He is a man of courage who is willing to go against the grain. He is a visionary whose life and ministry have profoundly impacted my life and ministry, along with countless others. He is most of all a man of God whom I love and respect.

*— **James Muffett***
Founder and CEO, Student Statesmanship Institute
and Citizens for Traditional Values

...

Bishop Ira leaves it out there for all to see and read. Not perfect, but a very empathetic and caring person. Hated by the devil and Democrats, loved by all who love God.

*— **Philip E. Hoffman***
Former Senator, State of Michigan

...

As an academician and former dean of Michigan State University's College of Urban Development, I came in contact with and was responsible for the academic success of almost every minority student that matriculated from public and private pre-university institutions to the halls of MSU—from our mutual good friend and successful businessman, Joel Ferguson, to one of MSU's finest and most prominent athletes in American history, Earvin "Magic" Johnson.

Bishop Ira Combs, Jr. was a student leader in the universe of Greek university organizations. While it is my view he pledged the wrong fraternity (Omega Psi Phi) rather than Alpha Phi Alpha, it is evident from history and his present success that he leveraged his years at MSU and ultimately in religious studies to pivot toward his extraordinary list of achievements. Ira worked in the College of Urban Development for a short season and while a student from 1977 to 1979. Jack Pitts, a supervisor under my leadership, was his direct supervisor and fellow fraternity brother (Omega Psi Phi). Ira left MSU in 1979 to pursue religious studies at Aenon Bible College and Indiana Bible College, finishing degrees in both institutions.

We later connected when my distinguished son, attorney Vincent Green, became a member of the church founded by the now Bishop Combs, the Greater Bible Way Temple of the Apostolic Faith, Inc. (GBWT). Upon our reacquaintance some thirty-plus years removed from his undergraduate studies at MSU, I invited Ira to Las Vegas where my precious wife Lettie and I were living and involved in the Las Vegas public school system for academic improvement of minority students.

The Honorable Ambassador Andrew Young is my closest earthly friend living from the days in which the ambassador and I traveled the country together with Dr. Martin Luther King, Jr. to spread the now universal message of equity, civility, and inclusion for all minorities, and access to opportunity to harness the American Dream of life, liberty, and the pursuit of happiness. Bishop Combs was asked to be my guest and introduce the Honorable Ambassador Andrew Young as the keynote speaker of the Las Vegas event. At this event, Bishop Combs and the ambassador reconnected from the work they had done in 2004–2007 with the "Working Families for Walmart" project.

Since their reconnection, the ambassador and I have visited Bishop Combs' church, Greater Bible Way Temple, Spring Arbor University, and the largest walled prison in the world on at least two separate occasions where the ambassador has advocated prison reform and ministered to at least 2500 prisoners in two separate settings. It was Bishop Combs's contacts with Governor Rick Snyder and Corrections Department Director Dan Heyns that opened the door to this great opportunity to bring hope to those incarcerated and seeking a second chance. Additionally, I spoke on the importance of education to a capacity crowd of young academics on the following Sunday morning of each visit.

In conclusion, it appears the life of Bishop Ira Combs, Jr. has been one filled with service to the community he has been called to serve (minister).

Bishop Combs, on the maiden voyage of your first personal autobiography, I am reminded of the words of my good friend and brother, Dr. Martin Luther King, Jr., whom I served as his Director of Education for the Southern Christian Leadership Conference (SCLC): "Not everyone can be famous, but everyone can be great because greatness is determined by service."

*— **Godspeed!***
Dean Robert L. Green

...

I became acquainted with Ira Combs at Michigan State University in 1976, his freshman year and my junior year. I was the president of MSU's chapter of Phi Beta Sigma Fraternity, and he was a neophyte in the Omega Psi Phi Fraternity chapter. Our relationship grew from friendship to one of mentor and mentee.

We shared a vision of institutionalizing African American fraternal life at MSU by establishing a chapter of the National Pan-Hellenic Council. This led me to advocate for Ira to become the

NPHC chapter's first president. He was successful in that election, thereby leading the first NPHC chapter at a major predominately white university.

Together we went about creating a strategy to increase collaboration between the eight African American fraternities and sororities—and the greater university community. Ira and I were successful in establishing and leading an active NPHC chapter that could boast of holding enriching events and of sponsoring a historic conference. In fact, National Pan-Hellenic Council President Dr. Charles Wright traveled from White Plains, New York, to witness the transformative effect our chapter was having on the campus of MSU.

During those formative years, the MSU NPHC chapter's achievements included:

1. **Representation:** Campaigning for a campus–wide referendum for the National Pan-Hellenic Council to gain major governing body status and a voting seat on the Associated Students of MSU board of directors.

2. **Education**: Racial Understanding Workshops between fraternities and sororities, held in the MSU Student Services Building (1977).

3. **Participation:** NPHC sat on the Clifton and Delores Wharton Enrichment Committee and played a role in planning the $17 million Wharton Performing Arts Center.

4. **Student fee allocations:** NPHC represented students of color in determining how $150,000 in student fees would be allocated by the Student Media Appropriations Board (1977).

I am pleased to note that I recently provided MSU's Historical Archives with our chapter's National Pan-Hellenic Council charter, along with a brief history of the NPHC chapter. As they noted, much is owed to Ira and myself for doing the groundwork from 1976 to 1980. Our work etched each of the then eight, now nine, member organizations of NPHC into the annals of Michigan State's Greek life. In doing so, we positioned the Black Greek community at Michigan State to fully participate in campus life and to have our voices heard.

And so Ira, while this was just an early chapter in your story, congratulations to you on writing an autobiography and documenting the many other professional and personal accomplishments you have achieved, my friend. Our views have not always been aligned, but our friendship and respect for each other will always be what binds us.

*— **Andre K. DuPerry***
July 2021

FROM POVERTY TO PROSPERITY

FROM POVERTY TO PROSPERITY

WORK HARD. WORK SMART. FIGURE IT OUT.

THE AUTOBIOGRAPHY OF

BISHOP IRA COMBS, JR., D.D.

FROM POVERTY TO PROSPERITY

Published by
Illumify Media Global
www.IllumifyMedia.com
"Let's Bring Your Book to Life!"

Library of Congress Control Number: 2022914027

Paperback ISBN: 978-1-955043-74-8
Hardcover ISBN: 978-1-955043-75-5

Typeset by Art Innovations (http://artinnovations.in/)
Cover design by Debbie Lewis

Printed in the United States of America

DEDICATION

This book is dedicated
to the glory of God
and graciousness in Christ Jesus.

CONTENTS

FOREWORD

I salute my friend and colleague, Bishop Ira Combs, Jr., for the release of his first autobiography, *From Poverty to Prosperity*. We came to know each other and work organically together for the mutual cause of jobs, careers, and economic opportunities for our urban centers when we were recruited and signed up to work with the organization Working Families for Walmart (Walmart Headquarters, Bentonville, Arkansas) at the training offices of then-CEO and chairman Harold Lee Scott, Jr. I was instrumental in negotiating with elected officials, bureaucrats, and municipal leaders in at least seven cities in the United States to expand employment opportunities for minority and underserved urban centers identified. Bishop Combs was the television and media spokesperson who engaged in debate with those who opposed Walmart's expansion, being featured regularly on international media outlets (CNBC, NBC). In my view, we were successful in our efforts for a season.

It was years later, through my good friend and brother, Dr. Robert L. Green, that I was able to reconnect with Bishop Combs in Las Vegas at an educational fundraising event for urban children of underserved communities. I was the keynote speaker, and Bishop Combs did the honor of my introduction. From here, we planned my visit to Jackson, Michigan, by way of the City of Detroit. It was my understanding I was coming to Jackson with three stops:

1. Jackson Prison to speak to over 1,000 prisoners incarcerated for a variety of infractions.
2. Spring Arbor University to speak to over 500 students on the issue of global civil rights and to join in a dialogue with my good friend and fellow diplomat, the Honorable Ambassador David Rawson (deceased), who did the honor of introducing me at the University.
3. The Greater Bible Way Temple (Jackson, Michigan), where almost 700 people sat to hear an abbreviated history of my personal work with Dr. Martin Luther King, Jr., as his friend and second in command during the tumultuous sixties.

The unexpected was on my first visit; I did not know the governor's office requested an audience with me. Bishop Combs, Dean Green, the governor's director of urban affairs, Harvey Hollins, and I were chaperoned from the airport to the governor's office. There sat around sixty local ministers in the governor's board room on the fifteenth floor of the Cadillac Building in Detroit, Michigan. Bishop Combs officiated the meeting, and I was introduced to weigh in on the issue of racism in the process of reviving Detroit from bankruptcy. The ministers were gracious. They listened attentively to my impromptu presentation as I tried to explain to the group the steps that I and now-deceased successor, Maynard Jackson, took to shepherd Atlanta through its bankruptcy more than a half-century ago to becoming one of the greatest economic hubs in the world.

We concluded this meeting, and I was led across the street to the St. Regis Hotel's Herb Strather Room. There awaited us almost 250 African American leaders of the Detroit business community. It appears that because Bishop Ira Combs was a board member of the Michigan Black Chamber (now Michigan Business League) and Pam Rodgers was the board chairlady, we were all seated on the dais. Here Bishop Combs did the honor of introducing me to this body of distinguished women and men. Once again, I extemporaneously gave a chronology of events conducted by myself and the former Atlanta mayor Maynard Jackson that led to Atlanta's successful economic emergence.

We left this event in Detroit and drove one and a half hours to Jackson, where we visited the Southern Michigan Prison (Jackson Prison). Here over 1,000 inmates awaited our arrival in the Robert G. Cotton Facility. I mentioned to Bishop Combs I felt this was a final chapter in my calling to minister because of the words of Jesus Christ our Lord found in Matthew 25:35–36: "Naked, and ye clothed me: I was sick, and ye visited me: I was in prison, and ye came unto me."

While the visit with my good friend and fellow diplomat Ambassador David Rawson was notable, my visit to see my brethren incarcerated was indelible.

Congratulations, Bishop Combs, on your first autobiography, and may God bless you to add many chapters herein.

*— **Ambassador Andrew Young***

ACKNOWLEDGMENTS

God in Jesus Christ

My wife, Kimberly, two children, Sarah and Ira, III,
and grandchildren, Autumn, Joslyn, and Joshua Jr.

The Greater Bible Way Temple Church, including
ministers, the official board, and administration.

The late honorable state senator David Holmes and
the late honorable state senator Joe Young, Sr., for
guidance in the formative years of politics.

The honorable former state senator
Philip E. Hoffman (Michigan's Nineteenth Senate
District) and the honorable governor John Engler
(forty-sixth governor of Michigan).

The honorable former congressman Nick Smith
(Michigan's Seventh District) who recommended me
to the honorable president George W. Bush for the
position of director of faith–based initiatives for
the state of Michigan.

The Honorable George W. Bush, forty-third president
of the United States.

INTRODUCTION

The purpose or aspiration of this autobiography is to accomplish two very specific outcomes:

1. To prayerfully and with painstaking detail attempt to "number my days" as written in the Psalm of Moses (Psalm 90:10–12). This, in my view, is my personal responsibility in the sight of God and in the *Chronos* (sequence) of time God in Jesus Christ has gifted me. It is unequivocal that Jesus Christ numbered his days on earth and in the days of his flesh, as well as the Apostle Paul in his frequent observation of his personal mortality, ". . . the time of my departure is at hand" (2 Timothy 4:6).

   Even Dr. Martin Luther King, Jr. was ever conscious of his impending mortality in *chronos* (sequence) of time God gifted him to serve the global communities' greater good.

2. The second focus is to prayerfully "measure my days" as interceded by the sweet psalmist King David and stated in Psalm 39:4–5. This would be the *kairos* (characteristic of historical events in epochs) or levels of achievements and accomplishments. The levels of elevation from faith to faith, promotion to promotion, responsibility to greater responsibility, poverty to prosperity, ignorance to wisdom,

receiver to giver, servant to sacrifice, from glory to glory, and praise to praise. Finally, from sowing to reaping and reaping to legacy. The measure of my days, or as the Apostle Paul hermeneuticized in Ephesians 3:17–19, ". . . to comprehend with all saints what is the breadth, and length, and depth, and height; and to know the love of Christ, which passeth knowledge, that ye might be filled with all the fulness of God."

From Poverty to Prosperity is an abbreviated autobiographical documentary and anemic attempt to share my journey from sinner to Christ and in Christ from glory to glory! It is my hope that some of those things shared will be edifying and efficacious to all who sacrifice their time to indulge.

To God be the glory for the things he has done and allowed me to experience, along with the local assembly of Greater Bible Way Temple, my precious family, the Northern District Council, the Pentecostal Assemblies of the World, the local community, and the global community I have been privileged to learn and share in growth and prosperity.

God love you!

CHAPTER 1

THE WORK ETHIC

At every age and stage of life, things happen that are out of our control.

But we *do* have control over what we do next. And what we do after that. And most importantly, we get to choose whether we let hardships, injustice, and abuse leave us crippled—or more determined than ever to thrive and succeed.

I am an average individual of African American descent, raised in a dual-parent home in an American urban city called Westland, Michigan. Westland borders Inkster, Michigan, on its northern border and Dearborn Heights, Michigan, on its eastern border.

I've been working hard, trying to work smart, and figuring it out for as long as I can remember.

My father made sure of that.

When I was five years old, he placed me behind the handlebars of a Toro lawnmower and instructed me how to push the mower while keeping a straight and steady cutting line. He warned me that there would be consequences of discipline if I missed a spot or left undone stripes in the lawn.

In retrospect, I don't recall ever missing the mark.

When I was six, my father decided it was time for me to join him in his landscaping business. When school was out, he would wake me every morning at 6 a.m. My mother would cook breakfast of commodity powdered eggs, one slice of bacon or a mackerel patty, and grits or oatmeal. We would eat quickly and leave the house at 6:45 a.m. headed to the Sod Farms in Belleville, Michigan, then to customers' homes in Palmer Park, Sherwood Forest, Joy Road near Livernois, and the Southfield Freeway area near McNichols Road in Detroit.

The Ford 250 truck in which we traveled had illegal plates and was in gross disrepair. I always found it interesting, however, that my father managed to purchase some of the best gardening equipment on the market. The Toro lawnmower, blowers, and walk–behind equipment were impressive. The jobs we did in the upscale subdivisions of Detroit included laying sod, fixing sprinkler systems, pouring concrete, edging, cutting trees, and clearing dump trucks of debris and hauling it away. The quality of work that he and my uncle Otis Combs did was admirable.

He worked me like a Hebrew slave and paid me with Top Hat french fries and White Castle hamburgers. Because the food at home was, for the most part, government commodity food, I quite frankly looked forward to working weekends during school and every other day in the summer just to get a decent meal from White Castle and Top Hat.

One evening—I might have been six or seven years old—I walked into the house completely exhausted and disheveled. I remember distinctly my parents arguing, yelling, and screaming at each other, my mother accusing my father of trying to kill me by working me to death.

My father laughed and said, "The boy will learn to work if he lives in this house."

Trust me, my father won that argument hands down, and the dispute only led to an expansion of my duties. My father seemed to think I was playing on my mother's sympathy, and from my recollection, I probably was. Unfortunately, it didn't work. Given his dominant and abrasive personality, it only served to increase my woes. He simply found more work for me to do around the house. One day he looked in our backyard and assigned me the task of digging out an inner–city garden by hand using a shovel and a mallet. My friends would come by while I was digging in the spring season and laugh me to scorn. However, I dared not fail to fulfill my assignment to dig out the trash–infested area, remove what trash I could, and plant tomatoes, cabbage, greens, green beans, and other nonsense. The garden was 1500 square feet.

. . .

When I was eleven, my father explained to me I needed to get a paper route.

He told me to figure it out, and I did.

I met with a neighborhood friend, Ernie Clark, and agreed to take over his *Detroit News* route. Ernie Clark was at least two years older than me and had an attitude problem. Nevertheless, I went to work with him as agreed to learn the territory. The route covered Powers, Eaton, McDonald, Annapolis Park, and Middlebelt up to Annapolis Street, which divided Westland from Inkster to the south border of the city of Inkster and the north border of the city of Westland.

Before long, I was able to collect money and create a budget to help meet some of the household bills. Every morning my supervisor—we paperboys called him the paper man—would drop the papers on my front porch on Powers. I would separate the papers, load them in a wagon, and drag the wagon up and down each of the aforementioned streets delivering papers.

There were always customers who left their "friendly" dogs out in the morning. Perhaps the problem was that none of these dogs recognized me as a friend. Unfortunately, when I refused to deliver customers' papers if their dogs were loose, they refused to pay. Obviously, bad blood ensued.

The Wilson family on McDonald Street had a dog named Flipper. Frequently they would leave him out in the morning, and invariably he would attack the paperboy (me). My mother was friends with Mrs. Wilson and informed her of my dilemma. This was, however, to no consistent avail, as Mrs. Wilson continued to leave this idiot of a dog on her front porch. I eventually decided to leave her newspaper near the curb of the street where I was safe.

After one year of delivering the *Free Press*, I insisted that all customers refer to me as their paper *man* since I felt it was disrespectful to call me a boy when I was being forced to work like a man. Most of my customers found this request amusing but attempted to be professional about it.

At the age of twelve, I expanded my interest in the community. As a student at Frazier Elementary School, I went out for and made the sixth-grade basketball team as starting guard. Mr. Grant and Mr. William Searcy were our coaches. The team stars were Derrick Mayes, Raymond Kennedy, Albert Jones, me, and a handful of others.

When my father heard I needed a pair of Chuck Taylor Converse All Stars, he went ballistic and threatened to kill me if I didn't quit the team and get a second job.

"You eat like everyone else in this house," he said, adding that because there were ten children to feed, I needed to learn how to work and do my part—as if I weren't working enough already!

Surprisingly and to my chagrin, my mother agreed with him.

I was forced to concede even after I had taken my own money to buy my Converse All Star gym shoes.

How ridiculous can they be? I thought but wisely kept those sentiments to myself.

Frankly, I always thought both my mother and father were insane. They were hardworking and had each returned to school to obtain certifications and bachelor's degrees—my mother's from Wayne Community College in registered nursing, and my father's in engineering—but their social interaction with one another and with me seemed dysfunctional at best.

After that disappointing turn of events, I decided that since I was now twelve years old, I might as well get a second delivery route. I connected with a friend from Annapolis Park in Westland named June Kimbrough. He agreed to sell me his *Detroit Free Press* paper route for a reasonable fee. My parents agreed that I take on this new responsibility and begin paying rent.

Around the time I began learning the second route, I lost my temper with my dad and was disciplined for objecting and talking back. After the beat down, I dried my tears, gritted my teeth, squared my shoulders, and left the house to meet June Kimbrough to continue learning the additional route.

...

Now that I had two jobs, I kept at least $30 cash on me at all times. This was a good thing because I was forced to buy my own school clothes and school lunches.

That Christmas my parents informed me that because they didn't have any money, I was responsible for buying anything I wanted for Christmas, with the exception of t-shirts and underwear.

I personally felt this was going too far.

I began to literally hate my mother and father. I even contemplated killing them, but after much thought of the consequence of prison, I abandoned those evil considerations.

That same Christmas my father informed me that it was my job now, at the age of twelve, to put up the Christmas lights in the blistering cold temperatures.

Every year at Christmas he would disappear for several weeks, sometimes not returning home until after the holidays were over. My mother was always closed-mouthed about his absence, though it was obvious she was stressed.

When I reached the age of thirteen, I felt it was time for me to address him on the issue.

That holiday, as usual, he left before Christmas. When our furnace broke a few days later and we had no heat in the house, he returned briefly to fix it.

He walked into the laundry room through the back door.

When he did, I was waiting for him.

"Where have you been?" I demanded.

"What are you doing?" he snapped at me, refusing to answer my question.

"I'm trying to figure out how to get out of here," I shot back. "Mom and the girls are all in the other room crying because you've abandoned us—again—for Christmas. What is your problem?"

He pursed his lips for a moment before answering. "I had to go away to take care of some business, and I need you to be responsible and take care of things here while I'm gone."

"I do not have ten children; you do. You need to stick around and take care of your responsibilities, just as I'm taking care of mine by running two paper routes and supplying my own personal needs."

He laughed off my words.

But apparently, he listened to me because that year he returned home in time for Christmas.

...

That year my father went to work for American Standard Corporation in Detroit/Dearborn on Wyoming Street. When I told my father I was interested in getting a real job, he said he would consider me helping at his place of employment.

I decided to give up one of my paper routes to Roy Johnson, who lived on Middlebelt in the area of the route. I offered it to Roy Boy (his nickname), and he accepted for an undisclosed price and a thirty-day training period.

When we began training, I always sent him to the customers' homes where the dogs were left out. Because it was dark in the mornings of delivery, you couldn't see the dogs until they attacked. I'd hand him the paper and tell him, "Now, Roy, I am going across the street to deliver to that house, and you take this paper to Mrs. Wilson's house."

Ultimately, he had to bear the burden which he did begrudgingly. Roy Johnson was a very tall and athletic fellow, but he lacked confidence. I knew this and found myself taking advantage of this weakness by bossing him around. Also, he could never outbox me or beat me in wrestling, so he would simply comply with my demands. Roy accepted the paper route during the Christmas season just before my fourteenth birthday.

By then, I had successfully built the *Detroit News* route from thirty customers to 120 customers and won a trip to Buckingham Palace in the United Kingdom to meet the Queen of England. After discussing the trip with my parents and my *Detroit News* supervisor, I decided to turn the trip down and take the prizes instead which included a television, a four-horsepower minibike with a Brigg and Stratton engine, and a host of other prizes.

That was by far my greatest Christmas in memory, with the exception of the Christmas following my conversion and the new birth experience in Christ Jesus.

...

Some people think my parents were too hard on us, and perhaps they were. My father often said to me, "When you hit seventeen, you are getting the hell outta here, so you better start figuring it out."

Yes, my father was hard on us.

Life was hard on us.

Actually, I don't know that anyone in my neighborhood had a childhood as we understand it today.

I'll never forget an event that impacted the entire community. Death was common in our neighborhoods, but the killing of Jimmy Matthews rocked us in new ways. In 1968, fourteen-year-old Jimmy Matthews was allegedly shot by the

Inkster Police multiple times. It was said that it was a case of mistaken identity but interpreted by all as police brutality.

We all looked up to Jimmy Matthews because of his charisma. He was, in a sense, a neighborhood icon. After this tragic event, the police–community relations, which were non-existent, worsened. And even though the Inkster Police Department began to integrate its ranks, the reputation of law enforcement in Inkster remained soiled.

CHAPTER 2

THE DRIVE TO SURVIVE

There were ten children in our family. Large families were normal in that day, and there were several large families on the block of 28975 Powers Street. Every household was on a level playing field in our community—except for those who lived over in a suburb known as Annapolis Park.

When I was twelve years old and maintaining two paper routes, I had expanded my business by soliciting other areas within the Westland area on the south side of Annapolis Boulevard, which divided Inkster from Westland and ran from Inkster Road to Henry Rough Road.

For the first time in my young life, I began to see some disparities in the quality of life. I saw that people who lived in Annapolis Park enjoyed a higher standard of living than those of us who lived on the streets of Powers, Eaton, Richard, and McDonald.

In Annapolis Park, people had manicured lawns, ranch–style homes, two–car garages, and brand–new cars. Their homes were like museums.

When I was growing up, Westland was predominantly white, as was Dearborn Heights, and segregation prohibited

African Americans from taking advantage of advanced educational opportunities in the schools of neighboring white communities.

At the age of thirteen, I entered Fellrath Junior High, which is now one of the many schools in Inkster, Michigan, that has become defunct, going bankrupt in the nineties. My mother desired to put us in a more advanced school system, but the boundaries of segregation prevented her from doing so.

My parents tried unsuccessfully on many occasions to enroll their ten children in better schools in the surrounding area. My mother, in particular, gave it her best shot. Using a fictitious address, she sent my sisters Ivy, Teresa, and Anna to Romulus High in Romulus, Michigan. She could not, however, hide the color of their skin and on short notice investigators showed up at the address she had claimed was ours. When they discovered my sisters did not live there, it brought about the swift end of my mother's "school choice."

Despite the indefatigable efforts of my parents—and my mother in particular—choosing the school your children attended was not a real possibility until Governor John Engler was elected and passed through legislation for urban schools to have access to the same choices in quality education as white suburbanites. This legislation included the development of the now successful charter school system in Michigan, which enrolls 149,000 students in 300 facilities, the majority located in the Detroit and Flint, Michigan areas.

By the time John Engler revolutionized education in our city, my siblings and I had graduated from our respective public academic institutions and matriculated to obtain post–high school degrees. By that time, I was out of college and a part of the John Engler school choice initiative. I was also part of the push for vouchers. I believe that if your children were in failing schools, you should be able to take them out of those institutional dispositions and move them into a more favorable setting where they can compete on a level playing field and thrive with other students in their class.

Unfortunately, of the people who lived in those particular geographical areas in Westland and Inkster, few moved on to be successful. Some did, but the majority (if you look at the demographics) proves that maybe 85 percent graduated from high school, but only 4.2 percent graduated from college while 11.2 percent went to college. So, when you have a 90 percent rate of individuals not going to post–high school educational institutions, it compromises the earning capacity and economic opportunities for those persons to grow and compete on a level of middle–class America.

I always held John Engler in the highest esteem for his Schools of Choice legislation. I knew firsthand from our family's experience the crisis that so many families and children were experiencing.

The schools in the Inkster Public Schools system were later reported as "underperforming," as documented in the July 2000 Mackinac Center for Public Policy article entitled "Conclusion: Competition is Improving Public Schools for Michigan Children." Eventually, the entire system collapsed. The Edison Charter Schools organization, under the leadership of former Detroit Public Schools superintendent Dr. Debra McGriff, took over to completely re-engineer and rebuild the institutions.

...

When my mother was unable to orchestrate a healthier environment for my siblings and me to complete our education, I began to realize I needed to make different choices from some of my peers.

The use of drugs—marijuana, mescaline, crystal THC, Turkish dope or mixed jive, heroin, and more—was rampant in my high school. When I was a ninth grader at Inkster High School, there was an outbreak of an epidemic of out–of–wedlock births. At one time, I remember counting at least fifty-five students who were my peers who were pregnant out of wedlock.

I knew I needed to come up with a strategy to escape this environment, especially since my parents made it clear that I had better not be responsible for an out–of–wedlock birth if I intended to live in their house.

I poured myself into sports. At the end of my freshman year, I spent the summer in basketball camp with Coach Grant and William Searcy. I also attended a program called Upward Bound at Wayne State University.

Upward Bound was a program for college prep students and was designed to prepare promising students for the successful matriculation from high school to college. We attended class five days per week from June until August. We came home on the weekends and stayed at Shiple Hall on the University of Detroit campus during the week.

Upward Bound was and is one of the most successful urban inner–city academic programs available for college preparation. In fact, it probably did more to prepare me for my future college experience than the classes I took at Inkster High.

I was on the basketball team as starting guard with the lead point guard Ronnie Fletcher. Ron was the real deal. He was a complete package player; I, on the other hand, was perpetrating a fraud. His talent was on a level equal to the best I had seen in Inkster. When our Upward Bound team played Cranbrook Institute and Country Day, we were completely humiliated, losing by twenty and thirty points. However, Ron Fletcher always scored his twenty or thirty points, and in most competitions, he led us in all statistics, including assists and rebounds.

We did have some unfortunate controversy while in Upward Bound. There was a gang from Detroit's Bruster Projects that wanted to control the course of events, and no one would step up and challenge them. I took it upon myself to represent Inkster, and a conflict ensued.

Neshawn Fikes, Wildred Hodson, and I confronted the gang members who were represented by a guy named Perkins. This was before every conflict was answered with a lethal weapon. Perkins and I met in the Shiple Hall lounge. He jumped in my face and commenced to call me a punk, among other things. I lifted Perkins from his feet and body-slammed him in front of all his friends. This only incensed the situation, and we all dispersed.

Big Jack, an Upward Bound supervisor who stood six feet, four inches and weighed 300 pounds, came in to intervene. He called all of us into his office, but no one would give up any information. Then all of us students reconvened in the Shiple Hall lounge, at which time Perkins confronted me again. Dale Wilfred Hodson slipped me a switchblade. Once Perkins saw the knife, he took off running, and that spelled the end of problems with the Detroit gang.

I was suspended for several days. Nevertheless, I returned to Upward Bound throughout my high school years. Sports and my work ethic were strategies for surviving and eventually escaping the urban decay of Inkster.

...

During my sophomore year in high school, my father helped me secure employment with City Building Maintenance, the company at which he worked, cleaning the American Standard offices in Detroit/Dearborn. The job paid $5 an hour, which was a lot of money for a fifteen–year–old in the tenth grade. In addition, I ran his landscaping business on the weekend, servicing approximately twelve customers in Southfield, Michigan. Later I secured an additional job at American Building Maintenance in Farmington Hills, working at Toys R Us.

I had more money than I knew what to do with, even with paying rent to my parents.

I decided to pay for my own driver's training. Because I had been driving illegally since I was twelve years old, I was familiar with the technical terminology and vernacular. I successfully completed driver's training, obtained my license, and began driving legally at age fifteen.

Just about everyone in the neighborhood who owned a luxury car trusted me with their vehicle, possibly because of the good rapport I had with most of these gentlemen as their newspaperman for so many years. Of course, it also could have been that I had seven sisters, and every young man in the neighborhood was trying to court/date one of them. Paul Childs allowed me to use his brand–new Grand Prix for the high school prom. Mookey Hister allowed me to use his brand–new 1974 Thunderbird for weekend dates. D.W. allowed me to use his new Cadillac DeVille whenever I needed it.

Having good–looking sisters definitely paid off.

...

In my early teens, over time, I had established a close friendship with my neighbor D.W. who was four years my senior. The following year, D.W. shocked me—and our entire community—when he became involved in the 1975 kidnapping of Timothy Stempel, son of former high–ranking General Motors executive Robert Stempel.

Apparently, D.W. and an accomplice, C.W., decided to kidnap a random rich kid and hold him for ransom. Driving around a high–end neighborhood, they spotted a teenager on a skateboard. After engaging him in conversation, C.W. forced Tim into the backseat of the car, blindfolding him and then driving him to a townhouse in Romulus.

During the ordeal, Tim was locked in the trunk of the car for more than two days, then released when his father delivered an undisclosed amount of cash to the Safari Skating Rink in Inkster.

Eventually, C.W. and D.W. were apprehended and convicted.

None of us who knew D.W. could understand how he could imagine—much less execute—such a plan. He had been a student at General Motors Institute (GMI) and a white–collar executive for General Motors. It was beyond any of us to conceive how he could be involved in a scheme like kidnapping.

Sometimes the most unexpected—and even tragic— events inspire you to take control of life and make your own opportunities, and D.W.'s involvement in this event was my impetus to strategize leaving Inkster. After watching so many classmates and friends consumed by the demons of addiction and criminal activity that were rampant in our community, I knew I needed to take more decisive actions to pursue a different path.

I told my parents that if they would help me move to East Lansing, Michigan, and allow me to live with my sister Teresa (who at that time was a third–year student at Michigan State University), I would finish high school at East Lansing High and matriculate to MSU to make something of myself.

They agreed to my plan.

My mother contacted her first cousin, John W. Jackson, Jr., who was the assistant attorney to Frank Kelley. He allowed me to use his address at 940 Bedford in East Lansing to get into East Lansing High School.

East Lansing High was a culture shock, yet one of the most enriching and enlightening experiences in my entire life. I was fascinated with the more than 204 courses of study East Lansing High offered, including several at MSU for advanced students. I met students who were taking MSU courses in the tenth grade. By the time they graduated, they were technically a junior at MSU in that they tested out of their prerequisites and entered the university taking their major courses. Inkster High, in comparison, only offered at best sixteen courses. The disparity was amazing. My only regret was that I did not make the move sooner to East Lansing during my freshman year of high school.

…

Moving to East Lansing was a turning point in my life. A world of new opportunities I did not know existed opened for me. Until that point in time, the majority of my social network had been African American. Now the majority of my network became Anglo–Saxon Caucasian overnight. Everyone treated me kindly, and everyone was striving to achieve success.

I was able to shift the focus of my energy from folly to planning how to capitalize on these new opportunities. I finished East Lansing High and applied to Michigan State University, where I was accepted with the help of Dr. Willie Ealey, PhD, a counselor from Inkster High, and his connection Joel Bryant, an admissions director who worked in the MSU Administration Department.

I've had people ask me, "How did you get out when so many of your peers could not?" Indeed, drugs and criminal activity destroyed the lives or contributed to the death or incarceration of well over four hundred of my classmates before they reached the age of forty-five. Police brutality took the life of Jimmy Matthews.

I think the factors that have contributed to my success are many. These are, in my view, the factors that helped me successfully escape the urban decay of Inkster, Michigan and embark on a positive career path:

- First, there was the God factor because ultimately, my exposure to the gospel of Jesus Christ in the summer of my graduating from East Lansing High and matriculating to Michigan State University changed the course of my life.
- My parents valued education. When we brought home unacceptable grades, we were disciplined. When we were cited for citizenship issues, our parents addressed the issue with discipline.

- My parents exposed us to Christian values. While we were not a religious home, we did attend church services on occasion and were taught the sanctity of life and the fear of death.
- My own ambition was a factor, as well as my choice to accept—rather than reject—the rigorous work–ethic training imposed upon me by my father.
- There were persons like Dr. Willie Ealey at Inkster High School who took an interest in me and made certain I and other members of my family were beneficiaries of the college prep curriculum in our high school experience.
- My participation in Upward Bound was a significant factor from the ninth grade through my twelfth–grade year at East Lansing High School. This exposure led me to understanding the benefits of getting a post–high school college education.

You may be living in suburban America or in rural America, but you can reach your dreams. If you will pursue the path diligently, there are paths to get where you want to go in America. There are all kinds of great American stories of people who have come from frugal and from very, shall we say, insignificant roots and gone on to be successful.

Take Barack Obama, for example. I know Barack Obama personally. I had lunch with him at the White House when President Bush asked me to entertain him, which I did when he was an Illinois senator. I don't agree with Barack Obama on social policy, but there is no question that he has a compelling story (made even more fascinating when the powers that be wrapped their arms around him and pushed him to the office of President of the United States after only 169 days in the Senate).

America has many paths that people can take. If a person has access to education, can get through the challenges of their formative years, and can get a decent foundation and academic training, I believe he or she can be trained to succeed by American standards.

CHAPTER 3

FATHERS ON EARTH AND IN HEAVEN

In the summer of 1976, Christianity was being introduced to me by persons from all walks of life and every denomination, and I began to feel the drawing power of God.

After I graduated from East Lansing High School, I partied from May to July in 1976. As the fall school year approached, I had been drinking and doing questionable things that made me feel I needed to change as a person. I had successfully changed my environment, yet I felt I was missing something.

Realizing God was not in my life, I made the conscientious decision to seek the Lord. I did not know how to begin doing so, so in late summer of 1976, I began attending several churches in my city. I attended Greater Love Tabernacle on Plymouth Road in Detroit, pastored by Bishop William Rimson, as well as New Creation Church, pastored by the late Dr. Lottie Glen Richie. While attending the Greater Grace Temple in Detroit, I was baptized in the name of Jesus Christ and filled with the Holy Spirit under the ministry of the late Bishop David L. Ellis.

At the same time, I was experiencing a newfound hunger for God; He was speaking to the hearts of other members of my family, including my sister Anna and my oldest sister Janice Spencer.

What none of us realized was the role that our newfound faith would play in very likely saving the life of our mother.

One day my father told me that he planned to take my mother on a trip to force her to confess to infidelity. He asked me to keep this plan to myself. My father was angry with my mother, as he had been for years. It seemed that every year there was a major blowup, and domestic violence ensued.

My sister Ivy and I had been instrumental in intervening and helped to reconcile their differences on a litany of occasions. I remember when I was eleven, my father had dragged my mother into the kitchen where he pulled a knife. I grabbed his arm and took the knife from him. Inasmuch as he was a pretty strong guy, he probably allowed me to do so.

Another incident had taken place when I was twelve. My mother had been out on the town with her friend Dolly Wilson. When she arrived home, my father opened fire with a shotgun. As my mother ran upstairs, I intervened to talk him down. I remember asking him calmly to put up the gun and stop the violence as we had to wake up the next day and get to school.

His response was, "Son, I'm not going to hurt your mother; I just want to scare her."

I think he was successful at that.

The violence and abuse seemed to be never-ending.

Now he planned on taking her out of town and confronting her. Knowing this would very likely end in violence, I shared his plan with my sisters Janice and Anna. Together we decided to fast and pray that God would intervene. We started fasting early in the week in August 1976.

On the Thursday before my father was to take my mother out of town, we gathered at the home of my parents to pray. My mother was there, as were Anna and Teresa. Our siblings Jackie, Ladonna, William, and Carla joined us.

We knelt together in the living room. As we prayed, God filled Anna, Teresa, Jackie, my mother, Ladonna, William, Carla, and me with the Holy Spirit, speaking in tongues as the Spirit gave utterance.

When my father arrived home that Friday morning, he walked in the back door of their little house on Shaftsbury Drive and discovered his wife and all his children praising God and speaking in tongues. The glory of God filled the house.

My father remained unrepentant, so much so that we sought the assistance of Reverend Fox, assistant pastor of Greater Love Tabernacle. When he arrived to minister to my father, my father humbled himself and was filled with the Holy Spirit. Unfortunately, he never fully submitted to the ministry of the Holy Spirit.

I had not only had a life–changing experience with God, but I had also seen him intervene in the lives of my mother and siblings. I entered MSU filled with the Holy Spirit and witnessing to all of my salvation experience.

. . .

Shortly after my orientation at MSU, I was recruited by Bernard Richardson, PhD, as a freshman to join the Omega Psi Phi Fraternity. I pledged and crossed with the line called "The Seven Executioners." Phi Beta Sigma Andre DuPerry later recruited me to run for the presidency of the National Pan-Hellenic Council to head up all the African American Greek organizations on campus.

I ran against Alpha Phi Alpha incumbent Jerome Barlowe and won, then spearheaded a campus–wide referendum to give the National Pan-Hellenic Council major governing body status as an organization. We lobbied all the white Greek organizations, giving speeches at fraternity and sorority houses all over campus. They voted overwhelmingly in our favor, and we obtained the status of the first African American Greek organization to receive major governing body status on a Big Ten campus, as well as a voice on the Associated Students of Michigan State University Board (ASMSU).

In my third year as a student at Michigan State University, I served as the president of the National Pan-Hellenic Council as well as on the following student and university boards:

- Associated Students of MSU (ASMSU Board)
- Student Media Appropriation Board (SMA Board)
- Fundraising board that raised $17 million for the Clifton and Delores Wharton Performing Arts Center
- MSU President Advisory Committee under interim president Edgar L. Harden (former president of Story Oldsmobile in Lansing, Michigan)

I had very little time to study, and my grades were suffering because I had overextended myself. Ian McPherson, then president of the Interfraternity Council, advised me to purchase a calendar. He told me it was impossible to get organized without it. I ignored him for a while and continued committing appointments to memory, but soon realized I could not remember appointments. This was the beginning of me getting personally organized.

About that time, I requested a meeting with then president Edgar L. Harden. I was serving as a student representative of the National Pan-Hellenic Council on his university board and thought to seek his advice on a career move. In the meeting, he was pleasant and professional, as I always knew him to be.

I shared with him my major (business marketing), and he suggested I apply for part–time employment at American Bank and Trust in downtown Lansing. I did apply and was hired as an installment loan adjuster working under Kim Currin and Ross Steckker. Apparently, I was successful in the installment loan department; after approximately four months, I was promoted to the commercial loan department. I was recommended for the position by department heads T.J. Maloney and Howard Haas. Both of these men went on to become prominent personalities in the area of banking and finance.

In the process, I came to understand the banking business and the language of finance, which proved to be invaluable to me in my future business and ministerial endeavors.

. . .

My parents were in crisis again. My parents and my siblings and I convened for a family meeting in the Cherry Hill Apartments at Michigan State University. In this meeting, my mother described the years of abuse that she had endured at the hands of my father.

My father was present, agreed that her descriptions were accurate, and promised that he would not ever abuse her again.

There was, of course, a subsequent incident of abuse.

It would be the last, as my mother had had enough. After twenty-eight years of marriage to my father and the successful raising of ten children, my mother moved out and filed for a divorce.

In the months that followed, I was the only member of our family to have occasional contact with our father. My nine siblings blamed him for the divorce, and rightfully so.

At that time, he was working at the Ford plant as chief engineer, running their high–pressure boiler operations, and living in an apartment in Romulus, Michigan. He was also going through his own grieving process related to the divorce.

Whenever I stopped by to visit him, he always brought it up, saying things like your mother this or that, I still love your mother, I'm still single because I love your mother, I never would have divorced your mother.

"Now hold up," I would say. "There was a lot of abuse going on there, Dad. You were out of control, and you acted violently toward her. No one would stay in a relationship like that."

"I was never going to hurt her. I was just trying to scare her."

"Well, you did scare her. You scared her right out of the marriage."

Once I told him, "The proper thing would be for you to apologize for all the devilment. You were the head of the family, the covering, and it was your responsibility to cover your wife and family, not to abuse her like you did. She'll never meet with you, never see you face to face—the thing to do would be to write a letter."

He eventually told me he did.

But when I asked my mother if she had ever received a letter from him, she said no.

...

In my third year at MSU, I spoke out against Dan Jones, who was running for the presidency of the ASMSU Board then resigned because of his openly homosexual lifestyle and advocacy. I held a news conference to announce my resignation from the board. This opened me to a firestorm of criticism from the MSU *State News* and the liberal media. The front pages of the campus and local papers criticized me. The local television and radio lambasted me. Professors all across campus ostracized me.

Eventually, I was the subject of so much controversy I could not attend my classes without being singled out by professors and questioned about my position. I decided to take one term off, moving off-campus, which removed me from the controversial environment for personal respite. When I returned, I reduced my class load.

About that time, I was working with the pastor of Christ Temple in Lansing, Michigan, Elder Warren. I was assisting him as associate minister of evangelism and church growth. And the church was indeed growing. In the eighteen months I was there, we grew from twenty-five members to 150.

One day he suggested that I consider pioneering a church in Jackson.

The year was 1978, and I was nineteen going on twenty.

"I don't know anything about founding a church," I said. "But I don't have any problem doing that if it is the will of God and I'm working under your supervision. Where is Jackson?"

He told me it was thirty miles south of Lansing, then added, "I will work with you, take you there, introduce you to Reverend Otis Holly and his assistants Sara Fletcher and Martha Brown."

We took the trip and met with Reverend Otis Holly and his staff who agreed to oversee the launch of a new church in their city. I remember them commenting I was quite a young man but they would work with me. They agreed to sell me a little white church building at 327 W. Monroe Street.

Pastor William Warren sat down with me and said, "Now you need to work on fundraising and see if you can raise the money needed to purchase the building. You'll need $7,000."

We requested help from the Northern District Council of the PAW who donated a portion of the down payment. We went to Bishop David Lee Ellis, who helped with the balance of the down payment to secure the purchase.

On my next visit to see my father, I told him that I wanted to start a church and was trying to purchase a small building in order to do so.

He agreed to loan me the balance required to purchase the building. He didn't say much beyond that—other than that at one time, he too had felt called to the ministry.

While my father had apparently resisted that calling, I knew in my spirit that my path would be different. God had revealed himself to me in such a manner that I knew I wanted to serve him with my life. My experience at MSU and American Bank and Trust had given me a solid foundation for success in business, which I would continue to pursue. But I knew I needed a foundation for ministry as well. I resigned as the president of the National Pan-Hellenic Council, resigned from Michigan State, and transferred my credits to a seminary to finish my degree in theology at Indiana Bible College in Indianapolis, Indiana.

My father passed away in 2004, and when my mother heard that he had died, she was initially suspicious. After the funeral, she confessed that she had only come to see that he was really dead. She told me she had no fond memories of him because of his controlling and abusive acts, and that after their divorce, she had continued to live in terror of him because of the way he had abused her during twenty-eight years of marriage.

I eulogized him, and the family was able to bring some closure to that chapter of our lives.

My father was a complex man. He was born into this world on March 22, 1927, to William Otis Combs and Anna Lee Reddick. A native of Michigan and the city of Detroit, my father was one of five children, having one sister, Ann Lee Reddick, and three brothers, Wilbur Brown, Percy Brown, and Otis Combs.

He was baptized in the name of the Lord Jesus Christ and filled with the gift of the Holy Spirit under the ministry of the late Pastor Horace Jackson, Sr., in Romulus, Michigan. It was through this encounter with the gospel of Jesus Christ that his immediate family came in contact with the truth. Subsequent to him receiving the new birth experience, my mother, Hazel Cummings, was likewise baptized in the name of Christ Jesus and received the Holy Spirit.

Despite his failings, some of which I have written about in these chapters, my father excelled in business and personal achievement, founding with his older brother Otis Combs Combs Landscaping Services and Combs Plumbing and Heating. Eventually, he returned to academia to pursue an engineering degree as a high–pressure boiler operator. To his credit, he succeeded and was employed by Ford Motor Company in River Rouge, Michigan, in supervision, retiring in 1991 with thirty years of service.

After my father's death, my mother, in her midfifties, finally felt she could go on with her life. She remarried a kind Christian gentleman, Lee Cosper. He took good care of her, and they moved into a ranch home in Berg Hills, Southfield, Michigan, where they lived as a couple for nearly twenty years until his death.

CHAPTER 4

HIGHLIGHTS OF THE JOURNEY

While working at American Bank and Trust downtown Lansing in the installment loans department with Kim Currin, Ross Stecker, and Howard Haas—and in commercial loans with vice presidents Clyde McKenzie, John Curry, Vick Loomis, Bill Siegrist, and mortgage VP Kady Haar—I was approached on the job by John Mansour, a credit analyst and workout specialist. He shared with me I should speak with his wife, Becky Mansour, who was managing the service department at Xerox Corporation. When I followed up, I was hired immediately. Becky Mansour was an affable and capable manager. Unfortunately, she remained in the job only eighteen months after my hiring, at which point she was succeeded by the most paranoid and defensive manager I have ever had the displeasure of working with.

Jim Green was an African American manager with an urban attitude. He was a black man gone wild with power. He bugged all of the employee's phones and monitored all conversations. He followed male employees into the restroom and waited outside the stall or stood by the urinal frowning and cursing. Arbitrarily he would call me into his office to interrogate me about my religious beliefs and refused to let me leave his office until I answered all questions to his satisfaction. This was unequivocally the worst employment experience I have ever had. It even superseded the abuses I suffered at the hand of my very own father while growing up. To make matters worse, he somehow concluded that I was interested in succeeding him as service manager, as he had handpicked his successor and did not want any competition. It was office politics at its worst.

He ultimately left Michigan and went to Chicago, where he was afflicted with a severe case of anorexia. This bout with his own mortality is said to have humbled him, although I never saw him again after officially leaving the corporation.

Jim's supervisor, Frank McKnight, was a man for whom I had great admiration as a professional. I ran into him at the Lansing Center several years after leaving Xerox Corporation and shared with him my extraordinary success since leaving Xerox. A few years after our encounter, I was informed Frank had contracted terminal cancer and had expired just a few months after his diagnosis. This news caused me great sadness. I had always seen Frank as the model manager.

I left Xerox Corporation after approximately six years. Despite my experiences with Mr. Green, Xerox was good to me and my family. By then, I had met and married my wife, Kimberly L. Marshall of Detroit. We had a daughter, Sarah, and we were expecting our second child, Ira III. Xerox continued to provide health care and pay me for approximately a year after I left the corporation. I always thought it was the favor of the Almighty God.

I signed up with A.L. Williams Insurance (Primerica), passed the state insurance broker's exam, and moved up in the ranks within the company, reaching the rank of regional manager. When it was discovered that my supervisor had been stealing client checks, the entire organization collapsed.

In the wake of that incredulity, I decided to resign. By then, the church I had founded—The Greater Bible Way Temple of the Apostolic Faith—was growing and in need of my attention full time. My years in corporate America had been good to me, but I had a vision I knew I had been called to pursue.

In the year of 1984, I invited a well-known evangelist, Naomi Sessley, to be our revivalist. She came highly recommended by our then presiding bishop James Archie Johnson. Upon my invitation, Evangelist Sessley came and was supernaturally effective in reaching several hundred people over a period of three years, all of whom had received the baptism of the Holy Spirit, speaking in tongues as the Spirit gave utterance.

The influx of new members and families had been encouraging.

But in one area I felt stymied. I wanted to make a bigger difference for people in our city at large, following a model established by my previous pastor and father in the gospel, Bishop David Ellis.

During the time Bishop Ellis was pastoring, Greater Grace Temple was one of the largest churches in Michigan, with about 5,000 members. Bishop Ellis and his church were very involved in the communities and city of Detroit. When Bishop Ellis saw a housing need among the elderly, he built an eighty-nine–unit senior citizen housing development called Ellis Manor in Detroit. When the community needed educational options, he founded the Christian Academy school. When the people he served needed financial and economic support, he created a credit union to help individuals and small businesses acquire capital. He was a member of the Detroit Police Commission and a badge–carrying member of the United States Secret Service.

Bishop Ellis was a mentor for my strategy of community involvement and community development. Watching the Greater Grace Temple model under Bishop Ellis, I envisioned what the church should be in the community, how a church should embrace its community, how a church should invest in the community, and the total contribution a church should make to its constituents.

Furthermore, my experiences in corporate America in the halls of our country's financial banking system have equipped me to navigate the challenges of creating a larger footprint of service in our city.

Unfortunately, there were barriers of entry to opportunities in the early days of my ministry.

I decided to speak with Evangelist Sessley regarding these barriers. When I shared with her my vision to serve our community, she asked that I allow her to pray for me. I consented, and the results are in the history of our success.

In the weeks, months, and years following her prayer, doors of opportunity began to open for the church and for me in a multiplicity of strategic areas as I was:

- Invited to head the initiative to integrate the department of mental health system in the Jackson, Hillsdale, Lenawee, and Wayne County areas, recruited by Benjamin Hayes, Senator David Holmes, and State Representative Joe Young, Sr.
- Named as the recipient of the first contract given

to an African American in Jackson, Hillsdale, and Lenawee Counties after founding Christ Centered Homes, Inc.

- Recruited to head the Ad Hoc Coalition for Fair Banking Practices in Jackson, working with the Asa Philip Randolph organization.
- Invited to serve as executive committee member for Pro-Life African Americans, recruited by attorney Bruce Barton.
- Invited to serve on the governor's clergy cabinet (1996–2001) with other clergymen: Elroy Sailor, Jim Holly, and Marvin Winans, having been recruited by Lowell Perry, director of Governor John Engler's southeastern offices in Detroit, Michigan (former Pittsburgh Steeler and University of Michigan All-American).
- Invited to serve on Choices for Children board at the request of Amway founders Betsy and Dick DeVos (1995–2005).
- Invited to serve on Great Lakes Education Project Board, founded by Betsy and Dick DeVos (1995–2005).
- Invited to serve on the following state boards at the request of Governor John Engler:
  - State of Michigan Child Abuse and Neglect Board (1996–2001)
  - State of Michigan Quarter Commission (designing the new Michigan quarter) (2000–2001)
  - State of Michigan Attorney Discipline Board (1996–2001)

- Recommended by Congressman Nick Smith and appointed by President George W. Bush to his faith–based initiative for the state of Michigan (2002–2008).

...

In the late eighties, I began looking for a way to actionize my conviction that people of faith should care for the less fortunate. Aware of a dearth of services in our city for the developmentally disabled, in 1989 I founded Christ Centered Homes Inc. (CCH), a nonprofit organization that provides housing, staffing, and personal care services for people with developmental disabilities or mental illnesses.

CCH required the convergence of my expertise in ministry, marketing, finance, building projects, community outreach, and housing acquisition. And it paid off. Before long, CCH was providing affordable independent–living assistance, personal care, and personal–development training to more than 100 residents in thirty-three homes throughout Southern Michigan.

With the expansion of Christ Centered Homes—and the growing opportunities to serve on various state boards, cabinets, coalitions, and committees—my dream of integrating ministry, business, and public service to make life better for the people of our city was being realized.

A pressing need in any urban community is the development of youth, and we searched for ways to make a difference in that critical arena, too.

Looking for innovative ways to change young lives, the Greater Bible Way Temple of Jackson developed a thriving youth program, Friday Night Live, which provides recreation and Bible instruction on a weekly basis to youth aged eight–eighteen. Most importantly, through the program, more than 600 youth have been baptized in Jesus' name and over 360 filled with the Holy Spirit.

The church has created a variety of programs for young people that have been very effective. One was a youth outreach program. In the late 1990s through 2000, LuBertha Oliver planned and organized a back–to–school program held at Greater Bible Way Temple twice a year for three years. Close to 600 students from Jackson High School attended every conference.

One year, we learned that a number of students had reached a threshold of several hundred detentions that needed to be addressed by credits, or they weren't going to graduate. The school principal gave students detention credits for attending an all–day conference hosted by our church. Students attended seminars on abstinence, study skills, career path planning, and personal finances. They heard from speakers about what a criminal record would do for your future and the disadvantages of felonies.

They were taught by top educators, including Ted Spencer and Nick Collins, two prominent African Americans at the University of Michigan. Ted Spencer went on to become associate vice provost and executive director of undergraduate admissions at the university.

In 1989, six MSU students started a campus ministry they called Young Apostolic Students for Christ (YASC). After a year of trying to self-teach and operate without a pastor, the students approached me and asked me to become the teacher.

Within one year, YASC had grown to twenty members.

As a thriving campus fellowship/outreach ministry and auxiliary of the Greater Bible Way Temple, YASC offered refuge and fellowship for those who have no watch-care, covering, or church while attending Michigan State University, or for those who are seeking to know more about Jesus Christ.

After years of personally overseeing the campus ministry, I appointed Elder Radar Johnson from Greater Bible Way Temple as church adviser/teacher of YASC. Under this leadership, YASC elected student leaders, created a constitution and became registered as an official registered student organization. YASC also hosted its first on–campus revival and musical concert with the gospel group Commissioned at the Wharton Center. In 1993–94, Nicole Young from Indianapolis, Indiana, was appointed president. Under Nicole's leadership, YASC held its second annual on–campus revival.

Sophomore political science major Monica Stephens from Niles, Michigan, was appointed president in 1995. Under the leadership of Sister Monica, YASC held a Christian conference entitled Christians in Politics at the Kellogg Center in Lansing, Michigan. The guest speaker was Apostolic Christian Coalition president Jeffrey Snyder from Washington, DC. His groups were lobbyists who worked to push Christian–based legislation through the White House.

International relations major Michael Nimmons was appointed president in 1996–97. Under his leadership, YASC put on Stir Up the Gift, a talent show featuring performances by several artists from the MSU campus.

Randy Meyers was then appointed president, and during his presidency he held the second annual Stir Up the Gift. The next president was Theresa Bass from Detroit, Michigan. Theresa held a concert at the Wharton Center with John P. Kee and the New Life Community Choir. In 2002–03 Jarrett McClendon was appointed president.

Deaf education major Crystal Hamilton, from Detroit, Michigan, was appointed president in 2003. Under Crystal's leadership, YASC hosted its first annual leadership conference.

In 2004 political science/social relations major from Niles, Michigan, Ryan Barr, was appointed president. Under Ryan's leadership, YASC's main goal was outreach and fellowship for the primary purpose of winning souls. During the 2004–05 school year, YASC held its first party "after" the Aud, an event geared toward reaching out to and connecting with incoming students. YASC also held a viewing of the popular documentary *The Truth Behind Hip Hop*, which was attended by upward of 200 MSU students. Many souls were baptized and filled with the Holy Ghost, and many others had a spiritual refreshing after this event. During the 2005–06 school year, YASC grew exponentially and continued to win souls on a consistent basis.

YASC also hosted a live viewing with over 1000 attendees of the powerful documentary *The Truth Behind Hip Hop 3* at the Greater Bible Way Temple with G. Craige Lewis.

In 2006 business supply chain Management major Robert Johnson continued the YASC vision of outreach and fellowship. Under Robert's leadership, YASC continued to grow in numbers and in strength. Again in 2006, YASC hosted G. Craige Lewis for a live viewing of *The Truth Behind Rock and Roll* and *What Every Church Needs to Know about Hip Hop*.

That year, YASC hosted two mini-series by then president Robert Johnson entitled *I'm Saved but am I Committed* and *Enduring the Trials*. YASC also started small groups entitled

TNT!!! (Thursday Night Thing!!!), headed by YASC adviser Ryan Barr for the purpose of creating spiritual bonds among the students of YASC. The leadership team also worked diligently to introduce the ministry's first bi-weekly publication entitled *Life Letter*, which outlined YASC special events, weekly gatherings, and other leadership essentials.

On the weekend of April 25, YASC held its first annual spring retreat and banquet, with the theme Are You Contagious? This was a *very* blessed weekend. Many were refreshed, and five souls were filled with the Holy Ghost by the conclusion of the weekend! Last but certainly not least, at the conclusion of the year, YASC counted a glorious twenty–plus souls who were baptized and filled with the precious gift of the Holy Ghost!

In 2008, broadcasting communication major Demetria Johnson took the torch and led the ministry with an aggressive focus on ministry. Demetria's desire was to see individuals' lives changed by the gospel. Under Demetria's leadership, over thirty souls were baptized or filled. Many programs and outreaches were implemented during her tenure, such as the highly successful 5 a.m. prayer and the YASC First Praise Break.

YASC also had the debut of their first concert entitled Stir Up the Gift, where Breath of Praise, Rock Nation, and the YASC praise team were featured. Under Demetria's leadership, the evangelism team was also revamped, and its name changed to Acts 1:8. The evangelism ministry took a much more aggressive focus on innovative ways to reach out to the souls at Michigan State University. To this day, the ministry of YASC is yet prospering, and God is still receiving all of the glory.

The success of our ministries and services was maxing out our facilities at the church. In early 1996, GBWT broke ground on new construction for a chapel, prayer rooms, multipurpose rooms, the I&SC Activity Center, a library, barber/beauty salon, women's lounge, and classrooms for Christian education.

. . .

On March 19 of that same year, Bishop David Ellis went home to his eternal reward. I count among his many legacies the profound influence he had on my strategy of community involvement and community development.

In his works on earth, I saw what church should be in the community, how a church should embrace its community, how a church should invest in the community, and the contribution a church should make to its community.

His was a model to follow that glorifies God in Jesus Christ.

And that's exactly what God, in His grace and goodness, allowed us to do.

CHAPTER 5

MY YEARS IN NATIONAL POLITICS

"Young man, you are a man on the move," State Representative Joe Young, Sr. said to me before adding, "and Senator Holmes and I won't always be around to help you. You need political coverage."

I was sitting in the Lansing office of Representative Young. He and Senator David Holmes had just helped me get into the field of mental health. They had worked hard to open doors for me to contract privately with agencies for which Christ Centered Homes, Inc. still provides supports and services, and I valued their opinions greatly.

I had served on a number of boards through the nineties under the authority and leadership of Governor John Engler. Now I wanted to get involved in national politics. Both Senator Holmes and Representative Young had earlier advised me to join the Republican Party of Jackson County.

"You are a Democrat," I responded, "and you are advising me to join the Republican Party?"

"You should do your homework. You will see the black folks have always done better under Republican administration policies versus the Democrats. In addition, eighty-six percent of all elected officials, regardless of their political affiliation, are prejudiced. Furthermore, you Pentecostals are too conservative, and your views will not work in the Democratic Party. Do your research, young man; the majority of black folks were Republican until FDR and the New Deal of entitlement programs."

The conversation ended with me agreeing to do my research.

I went to the library and looked up the history of the Republican Party passing of the Thirteenth, Fourteenth, and Fifteenth Amendments, the citizenship of African Americans, and the rights of women. In the history of partisan voting, it was clear that southern Democrats had created barriers for African Americans while the Republicans removed those barriers.

At the end of the day, I concluded that the principles of the Republican Party were more aligned with family, life issues, ethics, works, personal accountability, less control by the government, and more freedom for individuals.

A few years after this conversation, Joe Young, Sr., contracted bone cancer. It spread swiftly through his body, and within a matter of weeks after his diagnosis, he expired. I attempted to visit him at Henry Ford Hospital while he was in intensive care but was forbidden by his son, Joe Young, Jr.

He was given a private memorial. I often reflected on the irony of the decision to hold a private memorial, given that Representative Young was such a revered, prominent, and respected public figure. The turning point in my life's success is owed, at least in large part, to State Representative Joe Young, Sr., and to Senator David Holmes.

. . .

After the death of Joe Young, Sr., I met regularly with state senator David Holmes. We discussed mental health issues, politics, and religion. His sainted sister, the late evangelist Ethel Mack, was a licensed and ordained minister in the Pentecostal Assemblies of the World (PAW). She had been attending the New Creation Church of the Apostolic Faith near Greenfield and McNichols in Detroit, Michigan.

Her failing health made it necessary for the good senator to call on me for advice. I would come and sit in his office from time to time just to discuss his reverent sentiments for his sainted sister. After Evangelist Mack's departure from this life, the good senator requested I attend and participate in the memorial. We attended the family hour the evening before and the memorial at New Creation Church.

This led to subsequent meetings and discussions regarding his own mortality. He would often ask me about our belief in water baptism in the name of the Lord Jesus Christ and the baptism of the Holy Spirit. It was my humble opportunity to explain to the senator the plan of salvation through the gospel of Jesus Christ. No doubt, because he was a devout African Methodist Episcopalian, he never seemed compelled to embrace the apostolic faith.

It was only a few years after his sister's departure that Senator David Holmes, Sr. passed away. His memorial was held at the African Methodist Episcopal Church on Woodward near Wayne State University. His chief of staff, Anna Strong, was kind enough to include me as one of the eulogists along with the good senator's pastor. The memorial was attended by an overflow crowd.

Dignitaries who spoke included Governor John Engler, Senator Debbie Stabenow, Tom Turner (secretary-treasurer AFL-CIO), syndicated Radio One host Joe Madison, and I felt like a Lilliputian among giants. I read prepared quotes by Dr. Martin Luther King, William Cullen Bryant, James Russell Lowell, and others. The indelible parts of the occasion were the amazing accolades given to the senator by his peers, both Democrats and Republicans. All heralded him as a champion for the little man. There were unending testimonies by judges, lawyers, politicians, and community leaders attributing their success to the efforts, insights, and leadership of Senator Holmes. I sat in amazement and came to the conclusion I was one of the last acts for good works to his credit.

It was the good senator who, with Joe Young, Sr., opened the door of opportunity for me. It was also the senator who walked me across the aisle at the Farnum Building in downtown Lansing and introduced me to then–Senator Philip E. Hoffman, Sr. This introduction led to me officially joining the Republican Party and ultimately to my ascension to a player in White House and Washington politics.

...

When Bob Dole was running against Bill Clinton, I was solicited on the national level to join Bob Dole's national advisory board. I donated $15,000 and flew off to the Republican National Convention in San Diego, California.

I thought board members would have access to Bob Dole; however, I can't even remember shaking his hand. I did enjoy the convention, probably because one of his campaign managers was honest enough to admit that Senator Dole was not likely to win the election. Foreseeing the outcome after this mid-week convention briefing, I spent the remainder of the week visiting the finest restaurants in San Diego and jet skiing daily in the Pacific Ocean (arguably one of the highlights of the sum of all my political experiences).

The next presidential campaign for which I was recruited was that of George W. Bush. I joined the campaign team of Senator Hoffman and Senator Mike Rogers. We were charged with assisting Senator Hoffman in raising $10,000. We were successful, and my wife, Kimberly, and I joined the good Senator Hoffman in a private meeting with George W. Bush, Ron Weiser, and a handful of other dignitaries at Laurel Manor in Livonia, Michigan. The 2000 presidential campaign was off and running.

We were subsequently added to Governor John Engler's presidential task committee in an effort to deliver Michigan as a red state for George W. Bush. I traveled to meet Governor Engler for television and news conferences from Lansing to Detroit, then worked with Senator Hoffman and First Lady Michelle Engler to plan a presidential rally for President Bush at the Greater Bible Way Temple Church.

We rallied the local support of Jackson Christian School's marching band. Dr. Michael Bracy was so kind to bring his entire institution to support the president. Father Tom Reiden from Jackson Lumen Christi Catholic School sent a large contingency. The president sent the first lady, Laura Bush.

The event was considered a success. The church took its place in the history books as the first and only assembly in Jackson County to be visited by the first lady of a US president, thanks to Senator Philip Hoffman and Michelle Engler.

Prior to President Bush winning the election, we brought in Ambassador Alan Keys as the keynote speaker for our Conference on the Family. It was a joint venture with James Muffett of the Student Statesmanship Institute. Alan Keys is a very prominent intellectual and academician and one of the greatest speakers alive today. Quite frankly, he is a bit hard to understand; he's so intelligent. Nevertheless, he came to a huge response from the community. We also had Jeff Collins, who was appointed US attorney over the eastern region.

...

After the 2000 election and the controversy of chads were settled in the US Supreme Court, I was nominated by Congressman Nick Smith to head President George W. Bush's faith–based initiative for the entire state of Michigan. The interesting thing is that I had no knowledge I was nominated and approved by the White House until the news release was published, and I was contacted by the press. Apparently, Congressman Smith had been on a local radio station speaking in an interview from his office in Washington, DC when he announced that I was the new director of faith–based initiatives.

I immediately scheduled a meeting with the congressman to discuss what the appointment required in the way of responsibility. We met at his Jackson office.

"I'm hearing that I'm the director of the president's faith–based initiatives in the state of Michigan." I said, "I'm here to find out what that entails."

"Ira, I felt you were the best man for the job because you work so damn hard."

I smiled and replied, "But Congressman, what does the job require?"

"Oh, you are smart enough to figure it out."

The idea of the faith–based initiatives of President George W. Bush was introduced in *A Charge to Keep: My Journey to the White House,* a book he wrote just prior to his presidency. In fact, in his book, he tells a poignant story of an experience that shaped his convictions on this subject.

Shortly after he was elected as governor of Texas in 1995, state regulators attempted to shut down a highly successful faith–based drug and alcohol treatment program called Teen Challenge of South Texas because it didn't meet the standards of a "treatment program." Violations, they said, included frayed carpets and torn shower curtains. Yet Teen Challenge of South Texas never claimed to be a "treatment program." Instead, the governor noted, "it was saving lives through the transforming power of faith. Its program focused on Bible study and prayer and taught that drug and alcohol addiction were bad choices."

He went on to write:

What caught my attention was how ridiculous it seemed for the state drug and alcohol agency to shut down a drug and alcohol program that was successfully fighting addiction. . . My office stepped in and helped work out an agreement to allow Teen Challenge to continue to operate while we looked for more permanent ways to address this problem.

Texas has many kind and loving people who follow
a religious imperative to help neighbors in need. It
seemed to me that a government that truly wants to
help people should welcome the active involvement
of people of faith, not throw up roadblocks or stifle
their efforts with bureaucratic red tape and excessive
regulation. [1]

Nine days after taking office, President George W. Bush, through an executive order, established the Office of Faith–Based and Community Initiatives. Believing that faith–based and community organizations are in a prime position to meet the needs of their communities, the FBCI set out to strengthen faith–based and community organizations, giving them equal footing in competition for federal funds and increasing their ability to offer federally funded social services.

It was an ambitious goal. Creating and strengthening partnerships with faith–based and community organizations providing charitable services could revolutionize the way government addresses some of our biggest social challenges. I was honored and excited to play a role.

During the first four years of the Bush presidency, we worked directly with Congressman Julius C. Watts. He was the point person in the House of Representatives along with Senator Rick Santorum in the Senate. We were never on the White House payroll and received no reimbursement or compensation for our services. Raising funding from private sources, I flew twice a month to Washington, DC, where we met daily to discuss the strategy of education and implementation of the president's initiatives. The meetings were held in the East Room lower executive offices of the White House with Tommy Thompson (HHS), Mel Martinez (HUD), J.C. Watts, Angela Sailor, and Condoleezza Rice.

Congressman Watts's office was the designated war room. There we discussed an increase in aid to African countries, as well as strategies to connect institutions of faith and community–based organizations to available federal resources.

We also figured out ways to increase funding for traditional black colleges and No Child Left Behind, and were directly involved in influencing the legislation that led to those increases. As a result, under the Bush administration, funding to traditional black colleges increased an average of 25 percent annually above the level of funding provided by the administration of President Bill Clinton.

I have always felt an eternal debt of gratitude to both Senator Philip Hoffman and Congressman Nick Smith for connecting me to this once–in–a–lifetime opportunity of service.

...

The eight years from 2000 to 2008 were prominent years. We continued to host conferences at the church. Party Chair Betsy DeVos donated money to offset some of the expenses. Conferences were very diverse in terms of race and representation: Democrats, Republicans, independents, libertarians, people from community–based organizations, from non-governmental organizations, from faith–based organizations, Catholic Charities, Jewish League of Human Services, Lutheran Social Services, the Salvation Army, and so on.

A lot of prominent individuals came through and spoke for us. The keynote speaker for our Faith–Based and

Community Initiatives Conference was Les Brown, the famous motivational speaker. Congressman Mike Rogers, former chair of the Congressional National Security Committee, was another keynote speaker, as was Michigan Lieutenant Governor Dick Posthumus. Obviously, there were religious personalities, but there were also well–known public service and elected officials who came through during that period of time, including Congressman Joe Schwartz; Dr. Gail Beebe, president of Spring Arbor University; Judge Helen Brown, Betsy DeVos, Congressman Nick Smith, State Representative Clark Bisbee, and Dr. Jesse Battle.

There was a large amount of sacrifice. During these years, significant work was put into launching and executing faith–based initiatives, as well as into what GBWT was accomplishing in our community. In fact, at the same time we were launching faith–based initiatives, the church was building a $2.7 million sanctuary. The construction of the edifice started in 2000 and was dedicated on February 9, 2001.

After the building was completed, we moved from our gymnasium in which we were having services into the new sanctuary that seats 1100.

Our goal of developing our campus as a community asset that could be handed to future generations was being realized.

...

Working Families for Wal-Mart was a national program established in 2004 to 2008 when President Bush was in office. John Dunnigan from the White House recommended me for the position of spokesperson for the program.

Lee Scott was the chairman and president of Walmart for years. He was very well known back in those days when Walmart was expanding. He hosted a group of people—including Ambassador Young, myself, and others—at the Walmart headquarters in Bentonville, Arkansas.

During our meetings, he said to Andrew Young, "I want you to handle negotiations with the municipalities and the politicians so that we can expand Walmart in urban centers where Sears, Kmart, and others have left."

He then turned to me and said, "And we want you to handle the television interviews."

I was happy to help. I never received a penny for my endorsements. I simply expressed what I had witnessed firsthand: communities benefiting from the goods, services, and employment opportunities afforded by Walmart's presence in urban cities.

. . .

In 2011 Governor Rick Snyder was elected the Republican governor of the state of Michigan. I was instrumental in his campaign, then worked alongside him in the first four years of his governorship, my role including being appointed to a three-year term on the Adult Foster Care Advisory Council.

During those first four years, Governor Snyder and President Obama had an amicable relationship and pursued bipartisan initiatives in healthcare. Governor Snyder also focused on the turnaround of the city of Detroit, which he and President Obama pursued on a bipartisan basis.

Detroit had been in trouble for years as a result of a shrinking tax base, high unemployment, health care, pension costs, and budget deficits. On February 19, 2013, an audit review team declared that Detroit was facing a fiscal emergency. Governor Snyder accepted the review team's determination and cleared the way for emergency actions to be taken.

Some tried to say that because Governor Snyder was white, it would be racist for him to sign off on the bankruptcy of the city of Detroit. I believe in response to that, President Obama recommended Kevyn D. Orr from the Jones Day law firm to be Detroit's emergency manager. The recommendation was accepted, and Orr was appointed by Michigan governor Rick Snyder in 2013 to manage Detroit's historic bankruptcy.

This was the largest and most complicated municipal bankruptcy in US history. Under Orr's leadership, the city restructured $18 billion in debt and implemented a $1.7 billion revitalization plan that streamlined key city operations, helped improve public safety, put the city's art in a perpetual public trust, and avoided drastic cuts to pension and related retiree benefits. [2]

What was my involvement? During this time, I worked directly with the governor's Office of Urban Affairs director Harvey Hollins. I immediately set to work to bring Ambassador Andrew Young to Detroit to address the issues of economics and finances versus race and racism.

Because of my long-standing relationship with Ambassador Young, I was able to persuade the ambassador to speak to the business leaders of the Michigan Black Chamber of Commerce, President Ken Harris, the ministerial leadership of the Black Baptist Pastors, Reverend Jim Holley, and Reverend Keith Stallworth along with sixty ministers.

The ambassador explained to these groups how the city of Atlanta approached its issue of bankruptcy when he served as its mayor, stating that he and his successor, Maynard Jackson, were able to engage the Fortune 500 companies operating in their city to offer tax–exempt municipal bonds for the purpose of restructuring and refinancing Atlanta's debt. These bonds were sold on Wall Street and raised sufficient capital for Atlanta to emerge from bankruptcy, pay off its debts, and become an international hub to the global community.

From this event, we drove the ambassador to Southern Michigan Prison (SMP), where he spoke to approximately 1,000 prisoners encouraging them to redeem themselves. From there, we traveled to the Spring Arbor University campus, where he spoke to approximately 500 students in an exchange with former US ambassador to Bali, David Rawson. This experience for the students was historical and indelible. His final trip was to the Greater Bible Way Temple to speak to about 700 people on the subject of the history of civil rights and his work with Dr. Martin Luther King, Jr.

During the financial restructuring of the city of Detroit, I also worked with Director Jim Haveman (who at that time was the longest–serving director in the history of the Department of Community Health and former community health director under Governor John Engler for twelve years) to assist in the Medicaid expansion initiative for Michigan. I also served as a consultant for Fidelis SecureCare of Schaumberg, Illinois, assisting them in successfully becoming a part of the state of Michigan's demonstration project for the expansion of Medicaid-Medicare. Other health plans that participated included United Health, Meridian, and Blue Cross Blue Shield. Fidelis ultimately constructed four clinics for concierge medicine in southeastern Michigan minority communities.

Today, Detroit has successfully emerged out of Chapter 9 bankruptcy and receivership. Their bond ratings are a standing model of successful gentrification under Detroit mayor Mike Duggan. I'm no economist, and I'm no bond expert, hedge fund, or private equity guy. These are just the things I hear people saying about these subjects. What I do know is that Detroit bond ratings have improved exponentially. I know that now Detroit can borrow money at a reasonable interest rate and that they are attracting not only state, local, and national investment, but they're also actually attracting international investment. I know that Dan Gilbert, one of the richest men in the country from Rock Financial, has purchased over 150 commercial buildings in Detroit. He is the driving economic engine behind gentrification and economic development, and economic expansion in the city of Detroit.

CHAPTER 6

PASTORING AFTER POLITICS: EMBRACING THE ONGOING MISSION OF THE CHURCH

There is a verse in the book of Isaiah that speaks about the church receiving those who flock to it and having to enlarge her boundaries as a result which says, "Enlarge the place of thy tent, and let them stretch forth the curtains of thine habitations: spare not, lengthen thy cords, and strengthen thy stakes" (Isaiah 54:2).

Indeed, as the Lord multiplies the harvest, the church is asked to respond. And in many ways, that is exactly what GBWT has experienced since its inception in 1980. As the scope of our outreaches and the size of our congregation continue to grow, we have found it necessary to respond with additions and improvements to our church campus.

In 1985 we built our first addition. Five years later, we built an octagon–shaped sanctuary that enlarged our seating capacity from twenty-five to 300. That same year, we built a board room and pastoral office addition.

Six years later, we constructed an educational wing named the Anew Horizon Childcare and Development Center. We also built the I&SC Activity Center that houses a gymnasium, library, ministerial offices, barbershop, beauty salon, video studio, offices, classrooms, and Grace Tutoring, Inc. Finally, a beautiful, spacious, state–of–the–art sanctuary seating 1200+ was completed in 2002.

With every addition, we have asked for God's blessing on our endeavor. Revered men of the cloth who have performed dedications of the new buildings include the late Bishop Ross P. Paddock, Bishop Willie Burrel Sr., the late Bishop Harry L. Herman, Bishop Melvin Boyd, and Bishop Charles H. Ellis, III.

...

There is no mission more important than that of the church, and that mission is given to us to fulfill until the day of the return of Christ Jesus.

How then should believers and the body of Christ go about fulfilling that mission?

As I have mentioned, the ministry model embraced by Bishop David Ellis during his years of pastoring Greater Grace Temple made sense to me. Wherever he saw a great need in his community, he put wheels in motion to meet that need, whether the solution was "religious" or of a more practical nature.

Our philosophy has been the same. Providing services to the marginalized and the "least" among us has allowed us to improve people's lives as well as reach our community with the gospel of Jesus Christ. Some of the ways we have focused on helping the underserved include building a community center, operating a residential treatment center for inmates, providing homes for the developmentally disabled, and creating a housing development for immigrants and refugees.

In 2006, we collaborated with physicians and pastors and founded a chaplains' ministry where many souls have been ministered to in more than thirty assisted living and nursing home facilities. More than 500 individuals have been baptized in Jesus' name and/or have received the gift of the Holy Spirit. The chaplains' ministry exemplifies 2 Peter 3:9 that it is not the Lord's will "that any should perish, but that all should come to repentance." Many who have believed and obeyed the gospel of our Lord Jesus Christ through this ministry have experienced end–of–life salvation, miraculous healings, and deliverance.

While ministering in our own backyard, we remain aware of needs in other parts of the world and believe it is our responsibility and privilege to play a role in addressing those needs. On August 12, 2010, I was elevated to the office of full bishop with the Pentecostal Assemblies of the World, Inc. and assigned responsibility for the Forty-seventh Episcopal Diocese Kenya District Council. As a result, I served four years in Venezuela under the leadership of Bishop Edgar Posey and three years in the Dominican Republic with Bishop Moses Butler.

Our efforts internationally have included providing financial support to ministries perpetuating the preaching of the gospel of Jesus Christ in Kenya. Our support also provides practical help, making personal hygiene supplies available, developing a radio program in Nairobi, and distributing more than 5,000 tons of food in the city of Nairobi, Maasai Land, and Samburu.

Finally, we realize that youth in America—and particularly in urban America—are at risk, which is why ministering to young people has always been at the top of our priorities. In addition to playing a role in founding Young Apostolic Students for Christ, we reach out to young people with strong youth and community programs, including inspirational conferences and basketball programs. We reach an estimated 725 youth each month through our weekly youth outreach program, providing training and exposure to the culture of Christianity.

Finally, Master Peter May, who runs the community Tae Kwon Do program, has been with us since 1995 and oversees the training of approximately 100 young people every week. He has positively affected hundreds and thousands of students through his program.

...

Our organization (PAW) has rewarded and honored people who have been successful at church planting and church growth. If you've been successful in growing a church in a geographical area, you are elevated and honored. If you have been successful at preparing ministers, male and female, and commissioning them to plant or pioneer churches to expand and enlarge the borders of the preaching of the gospel and the footprint of the influence of the message of the gospel, you are considered a candidate for elevation to a district elder, to suffragan bishop, and ultimately bishop.

It is a model advocated by the organization. The organization maintains the exact same model that the apostles follow in the book of Acts in the New Testament. After all, the Apostle Paul planted churches among the Gentiles and the

Apostle Peter planted churches among the Jews, Paul being given the apostleship to the Gentiles, while Peter was given the apostleship to the Jews. It is in the organization's apostolic model to carry the gospel to areas where the gospel has not been preached and to plant churches in geographical footprints so that others can have an opportunity to hear the same gospel. Someone once said, "No one should hear the gospel twice until everyone has heard the gospel once."

Timothy Johnson lived with my family in our home probably for at least five years. He went on to graduate from high school and marry Sandra Johnson. He served as associate pastor until he was commissioned to go to Montgomery, Alabama, to pioneer a church there, which he currently is pastoring. He went on to be elevated through our Council of Churches, from there to an elder to a district elder, and ultimately to a full bishop where he has been planting churches throughout the south.

Rader Johnson was sent to Bay City, Michigan, to pioneer a church there which he pastored for at least ten–plus years. And then he was elected to pastor the oldest church in our organization, Greater Bethel Temple in Louisville, Kentucky, which he pastors presently. This historic church is in a Jewish synagogue on the Catholic campus of Spaulding University.

District Elder Philip Johnson, the son of Suffragan Bishop Rader Johnson, succeeded him in Bay City, Michigan. I installed him, and subsequently, a Baptist church gave his son a brand–new $2 million building. Both ministries are experiencing phenomenal growth.

Pastor Kevin Williams was allowed to go to Albion, Michigan. The Northern District Council had commissioned the building of a church in Albion, Michigan, which is sixteen miles west of Jackson. We had attempted to send several pastors there, but they were not successful. Then John Hemingway, Jr. was there for nineteen years, and he was marginally successful. He had a small congregation, he retired, and it was an open pulpit. We purchased this particular church building after Hemingway retired from the Northern District Council. We paid the council off, and Kevin Williams asked if he could purchase the building and try to revive the work in Albion, Michigan.

Pastor Williams paid off that church a few weeks ago and continues to carry out the commission of Jesus Christ as far as community ministry is concerned.

Then there is a church that was planted in Ypsilanti, Michigan, called Jesus International Ministries. Pastor Larry Clifton has since retired. His son, Alex Easley, has taken over and they have a thriving ministry in a brand–new church building.

. . .

When a man or woman is fully committed to answering the call of God on their life, they do not answer that call in a vacuum. Spouses and children are impacted, for better or worse.

During my involvement in state and national political campaigns, meeting the needs of a burgeoning congregation in urban America, and doing missionary work in Venezuela and the Dominican Republic, Kimberly has kept the home fires burning.

Graduation from Jackson High School with honors for both children was a significant milestone in the life of both Kimberly and me. After all, she had been the one who, during their formative years, sacrificed, supervised, and mentored—

not to mention transported them daily to and from school and attended all of their events.

Both Sarah and Ira matriculated successfully to the university experience: Sarah to Eastern Michigan University, graduating with her bachelor of arts/science in business administration, and Ira III to the University of Michigan, graduating with his bachelor of science in accounting and joining the US Navy to train as an NSA (National Security Agency)_cryptologist. Ira III went on to law school, graduating from Ave Maria School of Law in Naples, Florida. Sarah went on to marry, bear children, and pursue a career in real estate sales, becoming one of the leading sales agents in the County of Ingham, Michigan.

The role that God in Christ, the work of their mother, and the stable economic support provided by myself were unequivocally invaluable. It is with gratitude to God in Christ that I have seen my children embrace the so–called American Dream of life, liberty, and pursuit of happiness in one's personal journey.

I commend both of my children, Sarah Michelle and Ira III, for their spiritual and academic achievements as well as successful contributions to their community's greater good. I also praise my wife for her remarkable nurturing of our children and grandchildren. Her steadfastness and guidance have proven to be unique ingredients in their ongoing success.

It was Abraham Lincoln who said, "Always bear in mind that your own resolution to succeed is more important than any other. Don't worry when you are not recognized, but strive to be worthy of recognition."

...

When the Greater Bible Way Temple of the Apostolic Faith reached the milestone of thirty years of experiencing the blessings and favor of God in Jackson, Michigan, we held a celebration.

On the evening of Saturday, November 21, 2009, more than 400 guests joined Kimberly, myself, and our children at the beautiful University Club Atrium on the campus of Michigan State University. A godly atmosphere met guests and honorees as a professional harpist and orchestra ensemble rendered Christian music throughout the evening.

Honorary guests came from far and near and included keynote speaker Bishop Lambert W. Gates, Assistant Presiding Bishop (Pentecostal Churches of the Apostolic Faith), Bishop James E. Tyson and Lady Ruth Tyson, Suffragan Bishop Gary Harper and Lady Harper (Northern District Council), Chairman Pastor Steve Warman (Apostolic Church of Auburn Hills), Bishop Jesse Battle and Lady Battle (Bible Way Church of Jesus Christ), Bishop Moses Butler, Suffragan Bishop Howard Collier, and a host of other pastors, evangelists, and legal and political dignitaries.

After Bishop James E. Tyson led everyone in an anointed offering of worship and praise, Bishop Gates reminisced how First Lady Kimberly Combs and I have stood the tests of time, trusting the Lord Jesus Christ to lead us from faith to faith. He also humorously observed how, in the early days, I would preach to my small congregation of twenty or thirty members as if there were hundreds in attendance.

When I was given time on the podium, I encouraged members of the audience to be genuine followers of Christ and the apostolic faith, and to not be moved by the idolatrous times we live in that celebrate personalities rather than the Lord Jesus Christ.

It was a blessed event that celebrated God's faithfulness to our church—and to our family—for three decades and counting.

CHAPTER 7

REFLECTIONS ON THE POLICIES OF THE HONORABLE PRESIDENT DONALD J. TRUMP

In 2016, presidential candidate Donald Trump planned a trip to Michigan to tour the Flint Water Treatment Center. Prior to his arrival, I received a phone call from Governor Rick Snyder's office asking if I would meet with candidate Trump in Flint to talk about his various proposals.

I, along with attorney Jerome Barney and Alphonso Wallace, traveled to Flint to meet with Donald Trump. Unfortunately, the event was interrupted by the host pastor and SEIU (Service Employees International Union) protestors, and then–candidate Trump was forced to leave the event in a hurry.

He went on to win Michigan in the 2016 election by 10,000 votes.

At the Washington, DC inauguration of Donald J. Trump as the forty-fifth president of the United States, I had the opportunity to have a lengthy conversation with my good friend

Saul Anuzis, former chairman of the Michigan Republican Party and then senior adviser for the National Popular Vote.

We talked about the need for inclusivity right from the start of this new administration, and he shared that I was being considered for the State Department position of US ambassador to six countries of my choosing.

We met subsequently at his Lansing, Michigan estate with former state senator Philip E. Hoffman Sr., and later with Senator Debbie Stabenow and Senator Gary Peters, both members of the Democratic Party. Both of these historic statespersons were kind and gracious in their support.

After conversations with party chair Ronna Romney and national fundraiser Ron Weiser, it appeared I would have to live in the country in which I served as ambassador. To be honest, I was uncertain of my position to leave the healthcare company I founded thirty years ago and the church I founded forty years ago at the ripe age of twenty. While still discussing the logistics with my confidant and attorney, Richard McLellan, I solicited the support of Governor John Engler, who was kind enough to lend correspondence supporting my appointment.

I received official notice from the White House that my package had been received, and I would be contacted when a decision was made to move forward.

About that time, momentum on many initiatives—including my appointment—appeared to be derailed as the Russia hoax, charges of racism, and the George Floyd tragedy consumed the attention of the administration and the nation. These events unequivocally brought almost all initiatives in the Trump administration to a standstill. While honored to have been considered for service in this capacity, perhaps the outcome was for the greater good as I was able to remain living in the United States and continue fulfilling my responsibilities here.

Donald Trump ushered in a transformational period in media politics in that he controlled the daily narrative of the national media through Twitter technology. The national media followed the perpetual tweets of Donald Trump on any and every subject on which he chose to tweet.

Despite the fact that every tweet generated by President Trump was media fodder, a Harvard University study determined that 90 percent of the national media's reporting on Donald Trump's tweets was negative.

In my opinion, Donald Trump's Achilles heel was that he rejected long–standing, traditional Washington statesmanship forms of political engagement. He sought to clearly define himself as an outsider and to paint traditional Washington diplomats and statesmen as at odds with the American people. This meant Donald Trump versus the entire Washington establishment, both Republican and Democrat.

Despite the never–ending pushback and interference suffered by President Trump, the accomplishments of this president and his administration were unprecedented. Among those accomplishments are the following:

1. His conservative appointments to the US Supreme Court

2. His conservative appointments to the federal courts

3. His conservative appointments to the appeals courts

4. His tax cuts leading to one of the most prosperous periods in America's economic history, creating more jobs than skilled people to fill them

5. His attempt to address the issue of illegal immigration and illegal border crossings
6. His move of the United States embassy from Tel Aviv to Jerusalem and support for Israel
7. His hardline approach in dealing with China and foreign trade in holding China accountable
8. His success at moving America to energy independence and opening the Keystone pipeline
9. His championship of pro-life policies
10. His public support for religious freedom
11. His revision of NAFTA (The North American Free Trade Act)
12. His revision of the CAFTA (Central America Free Trade Agreement)
13. His revision of the TPP (Trans-Pacific Partnership)
14. His endorsement of prison reform to reverse long–standing discriminatory practices against minorities through our penal system
15. His early release of Mayor Kwame Kilpatrick

Other successes included President Trump's war on excessive regulations. The reduction of regulations in the arenas of energy and foreign oil, for example, led to America's independence and the opening of the Keystone XI pipeline. The priority by the administration led to the US emerging as the leader in petroleum imports, at least to the degree that gas prices in the US plummeted to record lows. Fracking suffered; however, US petroleum producers emerged as the world leaders. Unfortunately, the environmentalists cried wolf and declared a national emergency in carbon pollution and environmental contamination. These issues became political fodder for the political opponents of President Trump and exacerbated contentions.

The Trump administration also worked hard to remove regulations strangling small businesses and corporate entities.

The Trump tax cuts are credited with the creation of more jobs and personal wealth in four years than at any time in American history (see Department of Commerce statistics). According to the Economic and Statistics Administration (ESA), an additional 400+ billionaires were created in the US between 2016–2020. African American/Latino unemployment was at an all–time low. There were more jobs than people to fill positions. Unfortunately, almost all job gains were lost in the 2020 COVID-19 pandemic. As stated by Jerome H. Powell, the Trump–appointed Federal Reserve chairman, approximately 22 million jobs were lost in 2020 as a result of the pandemic shutdown.

What might he have accomplished without the distractions and interference of a pandemic? President Trump's own communication style, which invited conflict? The extreme level of pushback, bad press, and interference visited upon his administration by his political opponents? We will never know.

The Trump Administration and Religious Liberty

President Trump's fingerprints on executive orders that promote religious liberty and conscience–based objectives will be etched in the archives of American history. Historically, every agency has a civil rights office in the federal government. The Trump administration instituted offices of religious freedom throughout agencies in the federal government.

The Department of Health and Humans Services (HHS) issued the conscience rule that allows healthcare workers to refuse to provide medical services that conflict with their moral and religious beliefs. Though many of these executive orders will be challenged in the federal courts, a variety of religious denominations were pleased with the boldness of President Trump's positions, including Roman Catholics, Free Methodists, Orthodox Jews, Evangelicals, Charismatics, Latter Day Saints/Mormons, Muslims and Chaldeans, Pentecostals, and Baptists. In addition, multitudes of organizations that represent traditional Judeo–Christian values championed these executive orders, including American Family Association, Heritage Foundation, Catholic Charities, Catholic Social Services, and Lutheran Social Services.

The Trump administration held weekly conference calls with a variety of conservative groups. Dr. Alveda King, the niece of Dr. Martin Luther King, was a regular on these calls, and she occasionally consulted with me on politically significant issues. In conclusion, a list of some of the Trump administration's executive orders is found in the pages of this publication for the reader's reference.

The Trump Administration and Operation Warp Speed

While the Trump administration should be credited for its leadership in the COVID-19 crisis, and particularly Operation Warp Speed, the achievements of the Department of Health and Human Services, National Health Institute, World Health

Organization, Johns Hopkins University, Pfizer, Moderna, Johnson and Johnson, Merck and Company, Inc., AstraZeneca PLC, GlaxoSmithKline, etc., were mitigated and buried in the election quagmire of presidential politics.

A different and more harnessed/military approach was necessary to marshal resources, unify the health care institutional resources, and deploy the best and brightest to maximize interventions and reverse the spread and distribution of the virus.

The following is an outline of a strategy developed by Senator Bill Cassidy, MD, and vetted by Ambassador Andrew Young, Dean Robert L. Green, Lt. Governor Garland Gilchrest, and myself.

While portions of this strategy have been adopted, other actions—including the development of an immunity registry—have not been implemented at the time of publishing.

1. Testing for COVID-19
- Administering visible testing with accurate results

2. Identification
- Identifying persons with COVID-19
- Identifying persons who are asymptotic
- Identifying persons who test negative for COVID-19

3. Isolation
- Self-quarantine
- Mandatory quarantine, 14–45 days

4. Contact Tracing

- Determining when the carrier contracted the virus
- Satellite tracking the carrier's movement, 30–60 days
- Identifying persons that the carrier has been in contact within the past 30–60 days

5. The risk–stratified basis for return to normal orders state by state

- Remediation and successful return of workers in public and private sectors to employment
- Gradual phase-in of states based on empirical data demonstrating a significant reduction in cases and mitigated exposure

6. Immunity Registry

- The identification of persons affected by the virus that have been treated successfully and recovered
- Identification of persons who are asymptomatic but have empirically proven to be non-contagious
- Identification of those diagnosed with the virus but have developed antibodies to overcome the virus successfully
- Details of the immunity registry and its construction, training, deployment/ implementation are to be further explained by Senator Cassidy, MD
- The benefits of the immunity registry are to empirically track those affected by COVID-19 who have successfully fully recovered. The intent

is to mitigate the fears of the public regarding ongoing exposure and allow clinicians and health care professionals to track carriers of the virus for future treatment if necessary and as new interventions are discovered.

It appears, as stated, that the majority of these interventions have been adopted both statewide and nationally by the federal government.

Because President Trump's focus was on campaigning for re-election versus the virus, he was vulnerable to legitimate criticism. The rising crescendo of criticism ultimately undermined his re-election.

The Trump Administration and Israel

The Trump administration's position on Israel was biblically correct. The Trump administration's position to support the Netanyahu agenda was certainly a positive for traditional Judeo–Christian believers.

It was also morally correct that Israel is supposed to be America's closest ally.

I had the pleasure and privilege of visiting Israel in September 2019. The trip was an educational excursion with board members of Spring Arbor University. The hosts were Dr. Brent and Christy Ellis and the legendary Lloyd and Judy Ganton. We were fortunate to have excellent weather and a Palestinian tour guide in Israel who spoke a variety of languages.

We visited many holy sites including the fourteen Stations of the Cross, the tomb of Jesus Christ, and the Qumran Caves, where the Dead Sea Scrolls were discovered in the Jordan desert.

We also visited several museums, including the Holocaust Museum and the Israeli Museum, where the Dead Sea Scrolls are kept under guard by the Israeli Army.

Finally, we visited the newly constructed embassy in downtown Jerusalem. Moving the US Embassy to Jerusalem fulfilled one of the campaign promises on which President Trump ran. While it was seen by many as a controversial move, President Trump joins other US presidents who have made that promise. He is, however, the only president to fulfill it.

President George W. Bush and President Bill Clinton both vowed to move the US Embassy to Jerusalem, which would have put the United States in compliance with the Jerusalem Embassy Act of 1995. Since 1995, however, presidents have signed waivers every six months to keep the embassy in Tel Aviv, [3] claiming that moving the embassy at that time would create national security concerns and hinder efforts to bring peace to the Middle East.

Under President Trump, the embassy opened in Jerusalem on May 14, 2018. He also successfully brokered a series of historic peace agreements between Israel and her Middle East neighbors.

The Trump Administration on Foreign Policy

The renegotiation of NAFTA, CAFTA, and the Transatlantic Trade Agreement (TTIP) was a positive in foreign policy and trade for the unions who felt betrayed by the global elite. Trump's unilateral and protectionist approach, however, appears to be unsustainable long-term.

The Trump administration's rejection of the Iran nuclear deal was given some consideration by the Biden administration in that they paused to review the actions and conduct of the Islamic Republic and its supreme leader Ali Khamenei.

Regarding Russia, the Trump administration was forced to spend time and resources defending themselves against the Russia hoax. This distraction in fictitious foreign policy debate was costly for the Trump administration, keeping the perception of political corruption before the people, while convoluting the real facts concerning Russia and the so-called Russia hoax.

The Trump Administration and the Courts

Because President Trump was able to successfully appoint more than 200 judges to the federal bench and three justices to the US Supreme Court, he probably will go down in history as one of the most successful presidents to serve using distraction to achieve a clear strategic political end.

This includes fifty-four appeals court judges and 174 District Court Judges, for a total of 228 jurists of the constructionist federalist persuasion, willing to interpret the law rather than using the bench as a legislative tool.

It is clear from historical facts that several presidents over their two-term tenure appointed more judges than President Trump appointed in his one term in office. For example, Barack Obama made 320 appointments, George W. Bush made 322 appointments, Bill Clinton made 367 appointments, and Ronald Reagan made 358 appointments.

President Trump's three Supreme Court appointments, however, exceed the number appointed by any president since Ronald Reagan.

Yet, the course of history will, in part, be determined by law and policy in government.

The Trump Administration Immigration

The Trump administration appears to have law and policy on its side on this issue. The necessity to enforce the law, build a wall to assist enforcement, and work legislatively on a path to citizenship for immigrants is, in my view, an urgent matter. The porous borders of the US need to be addressed with a bipartisan solution by a bipartisan body of leaders.

President Trump's approach was working. His administration built more than 400 miles of border wall, reducing illegal crossings in those regions by 87 percent.[4] His policies also ended the deadly "catch and release," which allowed those detained while crossing illegally to be returned to their home countries.

A detailed list of actions taken by the Trump administration to stem illegal immigration can be found in Appendix A.

What Could Trump Have Done Differently?

While President Trump generated and received unprecedented pushback and negative media spin, his policies are perceived by many to have been good for America.

What could he have done differently to reduce his political exposure and perhaps win a second term in office? I propose the following four pivots:

1. He should have pivoted in his communication
    to focus on developing an Evolving Report Card

outlining his success on "promises made, promises kept."

2. He should have mitigated off–script statements that involved radical responses and unnecessary objections, starting fires with no relevant outcome.

3. He should have presented himself as a disciplined leader, marshaling all of the world's finest resources to fight the COVID-19 pandemic and ordering a bipartisan response in a tumultuous election year.

4. He should have stayed on message, focusing on achievements and proposals for the next four years to bring the country together.

In conclusion, if President Trump had been more selective in picking and choosing his battles and measured in communicating his tweets, he could have no doubt mitigated his political exposure and possibly won a second term.

$$\overline{\text{CHAPTER 8}}$$

REFLECTIONS ON GEOPOLITICAL ISSUES CONCERNING CHINA

A chorus of voices is recommending the US rethink its approach to China. Kurt M. Campbell and Ely Ratner, in their article entitled "The China Reckoning: How Beijing Defied American Expectations,"[5] make a variety of cogent observations regarding the need to rethink US foreign policy with China. They note American strategy to instigate political liberalization has failed to materialize. "Rapprochement" was supposed "to spark economic development, the creation of a middle class demanding new rights and legal reforms that would necessitate further progress." Promising signs of this metamorphosis are said to have seemed certain "after the collapse of the Soviet Union and democratic transition of South Korea and Taiwan." The proclamation of President George H.W. Bush heralded US policy in China.[6] Campbell and Ratner state, "US policy aimed to facilitate this process by sharing technology, furthering trade and investment, promoting people–to–people exchanges and admitting hundreds of thousands of Chinese students to American universities." Quite to the contrary has China responded (as noted by Campbell and Ratner).

It seems evident that as a result of the fall of the Soviet Union, China has adopted a "survival of the fittest" approach to globalization and constructed more barriers of entry to its markets, tightened state/central government control, constricting rather than reinforcing the free flow of people, ideas, and commerce. The conclusion appears to be at this time "events of the last decade have dashed even modest hopes for (China's) political liberalization."[7]

Finally, China has been anemic in its response to the nuclear aggression of North Korea's Kim Jong-Un. While policymakers and academicians assumed China would learn from the fall of the Soviet Union and change course in challenging the US as a military power, China, on the other hand, has chosen to compete. Xi Jinping is now ascending to the ranks of Mao Tse-tung in power and has set out to build a world–class military of its own, accelerating the modernization of the People's Liberation Army (PLA) while failing to enforce trade embargo sanctions against North Korea to dissuade their nuclear proliferation ambitions of aggression.

In conclusion, the US will need to refocus its efforts on US–Chinese global strategy to mitigate China's agenda for global dominance. As China sets out to expand its geopolitical footprint and build its own set of regional and international institutions, US policy should seek to mitigate displacement of US interest, especially on the continent of Africa, where US foreign aid is tied to democratic governance reforms.

Sociologists and archaeologists have researched the phenomenon of racism for the past sixty years. They are in agreement that race is a social construct versus a biological phenomenon.

This, no doubt, is because all races have all things in common as homo sapiens. And, from a biological disposition, all races are homogeneous to such an extent that the only physiological barrier that differentiates us as a people is blood type, which has nothing scientifically to do with one's race/color.

As a social construct, racial barriers were historically constructed with destructive consequences to their victims. This is in part because laws, statutes, and public and private policies as well as practices gave privilege to the race in power. Such was the case in South Africa as well as Namibia prior to their emancipation from colonial rule. The artificial construction of the aforementioned barriers was justified, in part, to preserve and perpetuate perceived superior cultural norms, as well as the successful economic system of productivity that the social construct engendered.

The abolition of apartheid in South Africa—the deconstruction of a constitution that engendered racism in the framework of the nation's legal structure—was South Africa's repentance. The construction of a new constitution under President Nelson Mandela, giving equal rights and privileges to all regardless of race, creed, color, gender, and sexual orientation, was the nation's act of faith in the long-standing principles of democracy. However, this has led Western nations to become politically complacent in their quest to democratize the continent of Africa. The US and its allies' complacency is also responsible part and parcel for the rise of China's influence in Africa and its exploitation of past negative social constructs (apartheid) coupled with their leader, Xi Jinping, aligning himself with Russia and pursuing a course which belies "a range of American expectations" first introduced in President Richard M. Nixon's rapprochement strategy almost fifty years ago.

Positive democratic, inclusive social constructs in African nations, coupled with enforcement of UN policy dissuading African nations that receive foreign aid from the US and/or its allies from doing business with North Korea, is critical to the US's continued expanded interest and success in Africa.

During these tumultuous geopolitical times where differences between the United States and China are exacerbated by the insane acts of North Korean dictator Kim Jong-un, the involvement of China/North Korea in the political–economic and historical constructs of Namibia are intrinsically problematic both short and long-term, particularly for the following reasons:

American and Chinese civilizations are culturally diametrically opposite in their view of the world and values of their citizenry. This observation is probably oversimplified in the essay penned by Samuel Huntington, "The Clash of Civilizations." In this writing, Huntington describes the gulf between US–led Western and Chinese civilizations as "just as deep and enduringly consequential as the divide between Western and Islamic civilization." In Huntington's words, "The very notion that there could be 'a universal civilization' is a Western idea, directly at odds with the particularism of most Asian societies and their emphasis on what distinguishes one people from another." He states tensions between American and Chinese values, traditions, and philosophies will aggravate fundamental structural stresses that occur when a rising power such as China threatens to displace an established power such as the United States. This keen observation is reversed in terms of influence in Namibia, inasmuch as the dominant economic influence relative to borrowing seems to exist between China and Namibia versus the United States.[8] However, the trade relationship between Namibia and North Korea versus the United States appears to give the US a competitive advantage, with our nation's annual trade approximately $400 million–plus compared to approximately $7 million between North Korea and Namibia.

Additional observations of Huntington are the divergent views of government between the US and China. He notes Americans see government as a necessary evil and believe the states' tendency toward tyranny and abuse of power must be feared and constrained. The Chinese, on the other hand, view it as a necessary good, the fundamental pillar ensuring order and preventing chaos. Chinese culture does not celebrate American–style individualism, which measures society by how well it protects the rights and fosters the freedom of individuals. It is said in China, "Order is the highest value and harmony results from a hierarchy in which participants obey Confucius' first imperative: Know thy place." This view applies not only to domestic society but also to global affairs where the Chinese view holds that China's rightful place is atop the pyramid; other states should be arranged as subordinate tributaries. Unequivocally, this philosophy is inculcated to some degree in the North Korean sociopolitical psyche.

On the subject of Chinese exceptionalism, it has been observed by scholar and historian Harry Gelber that the Chinese see themselves as the center of the universe.[9] Even Chinese Xi Jinping declares in his 2014 published work, *The Governance of China*, that "China's continuous civilization is not equal to anything on earth, but a unique achievement in world history." Quite to the contrary, Americans see themselves as well as exceptional and beacons of freedom, bulwarks of civilization and champions of democracy. The Declaration of Independence, Constitution, Bill of Rights, and Emancipation Proclamation speak these ends, not to mention the longest-standing successful democracy in the history of civilization.

In contrast, as noted by Allison, we declare *e pluribus unum* (out of many, we are one). If North Korean influence and Chinese investment continue in Namibia and expand, they obviously pose a competitive challenge to all outsiders. Finally, because China's view of time and experience will ensure their long-term commitment to expansion, as the Chinese are found to be more historical-minded and often think in terms of decades and even centuries, as noted by Graham Allison, the geopolitical and economic relationship with the United States and its Western allies will undoubtedly become more complex to navigate.

CHAPTER 9

REFLECTIONS ON CRITICAL RACE THEORY

In my view, critical race theory is an ill–conceived ideology from the liberal secular progressives to divert attention from the research and revelation of historical facts surrounding race, slavery, discrimination, bigotry, hatred, and violence that have been buried in America's ugly past.

While I do not profess to be an expert in sociology or on the subject of race, my commentaries are the perceptions of an observationist who has experienced a reasonable degree of systemic discrimination and has been exposed to an introductory academic assessment of its effects.

The proper approach is to commission all academic institutions to teach the sum of all American history and its dealings with all races and ethnicities in the past. This includes:

1. Slavery
2. Black codes
3. Jim Crow laws
4. The KKK

5. The Knights of the White Camelia
6. Massacre in Oklahoma, Black Wall Street
7. The work of abolitionists, elected officials, activists, and Christians to end slavery
8. The work of civil rights activists, politics, and religious leaders of all persuasions to eradicate segregation, prejudice, discrimination, bigotry, and implicit bias in contemporary Western society and culture

As well as the positive contributions of blacks and other minorities:

1. Inventors
2. Military heroes
3. Sports heroes
4. Educators
5. Engineers
6. Politicians
7. Scientists

We do not need critical race theory as we are far beyond theory in race relations and deep into application. Therefore, we need critical race history to teach the facts of the history of race and pose solutions to avoid future atrocities; as we well know, those who forget history are doomed to repeat it.

*Historical picture. This photo was taken during the
president's first four years in office and prior to the 9/11
attacks on the World Trade Center towers. The president had
just completed a five–nation tour of the continent of Africa to
promote his foreign aid to fight the global epidemic of AIDS/
HIV. In this photo: Bishop Ira Combs, Jr., Bishop Gilbert E.
Patterson (then presiding President of COGIC), nationally
known pastor Dr. Tony Evans, and representatives from
the Catholic Church and the Salvation Army. We greeted
the president in the Oval Office and posed for photos in the
Eisenhour executive wing of the White House. The president
then announced his administration's $25 million initiative
as a down payment to five African nations to assist in their
fight against the AIDS epidemic.*

Congressman Dick Armey, Bishop Ira Combs, and Congressman Nick Smith attending a fundraiser to support Congressman Smith's campaign

Ira Combs and former first lady Barbara Bush at a fundraiser for George W. Bush's 2000 campaign held at the Frank Lloyd Wright mansion of Tom Monaghan in Ann Arbor, Michigan

At the Lansing Country Club in 1999: Congressman Fred Upton, Pete Hoekstra, Senator Spence Abraham, Congressman Nick Smith, Bishop Ira Combs, Jr., Governor John Engler, Congressman Joe Knollenberg, and Congressman Dave Camp

Bishop Ira Combs and Senator Barack Obama at a White House luncheon in 2004

*Bishop Ira Combs and US House of Representatives Speaker
of the House Newt Gingrich*

*Bishop Ira Combs, Jr., Vice President Dick Cheney, and
Senator Mike Rogers (Brighton, Michigan, 2001)*

This particular photo was taken during the first term of President Barack Obama. The meeting was held in Grand Rapids, Michigan, at the Amway Grand Hotel, followed by a private strategy session in the Presidential Suite of the Amway Grand Hotel. The meeting was facilitated by Richard DeVos, Sr., and the keynote speaker was Congressman John Boehner.

Bishop Ira Combs, Jr., Congressman J.C. Watts, and Congressman Nick Smith at the Smith estate in Addison, Michigan

Governor John Engler and students from MSU at a rally
held at Greater Bible Way Temple, Jackson, Michigan

The Right Reverend James Hines, Bishop Ira Combs, Jr., and GOP Party Chair Betsy DeVos at Greater Bible Way Temple to promote school choice (2004)

Presiding Bishop Charles Ellis III, Bishop and Lady
Kimberly Combs presiding over the installation of Bishop
Combs over the Fifth Episcopal Diocese of the PAW (2014)

Dean Robert L. Greene, PhD (former dean of the College of Urban Development, MSU, and former director of the Southern Christian Leadership Conference Education Department under Dr. Martin Luther King Jr.) speaking at the installation of Bishop Combs (2014)

The legendary Bill Brooks, Sr., former vice president of General Motors Corporation, speaking at the installation of Bishop Combs (2014)

*The Honorable Richard McLellan (chief legal counsel
to Governor William Milliken, Governor John Engler,
Governor Rick Snyder, and adviser to Governor Gretchen
Whitmer) speaking at the elevation*

Elroy Sailor (former director of urban affairs for the state of Michigan under Governor John Engler, assistant director of national faith–based initiatives under President George W. Bush, out of the office of Congressman Julius Caesar Watts) speaking at the elevation (2014)

The distinguished Charles Ellis IV escorting First Lady Kimberly Combs, participating in the sacrament of consecration

*Jackson County Sheriff Steve Rand speaking at the
installation of Bishop Combs (2014)*

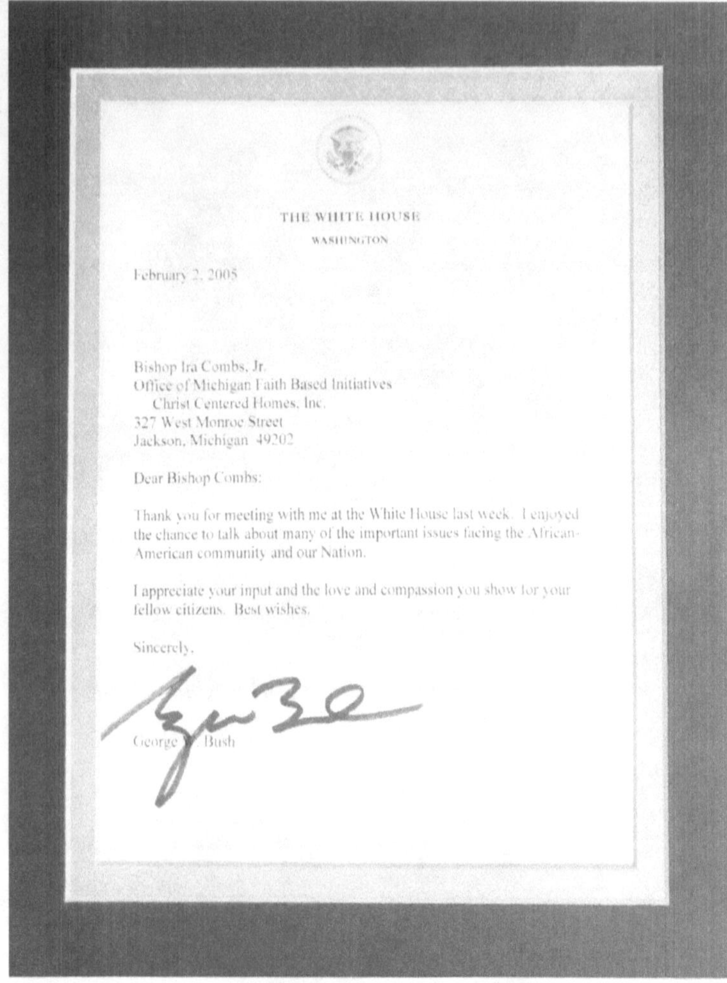

THE WHITE HOUSE

WASHINGTON

February 2, 2005

Bishop Ira Combs, Jr.
Office of Michigan Faith Based Initiatives
    Christ Centered Homes, Inc.
327 West Monroe Street
Jackson, Michigan 49202

Dear Bishop Combs:

Thank you for meeting with me at the White House last week. I enjoyed the chance to talk about many of the important issues facing the African-American community and our Nation.

I appreciate your input and the love and compassion you show for your fellow citizens. Best wishes.

Sincerely,

George W. Bush

Faith–based initiative letter from President George W. Bush

*Bishop Ira Combs, Jr., and Ambassador Andrew Young
during Black History Week at the Greater Bible Way Temple
(2012)*

Standing: Bishop Ira Combs, Jr., and Dr. Robert L. Green
Seated: Congressman Tim Walberg, Ambassador Andrew
Young, and Ambassador David Rawson

*Associate Pastor Dennis Treadway, musical artist
John P. Kee, and Bishop Ira Combs, Jr. at the MSU Wharton
Center concert hosted by Greater Bible Way Temple*

Crowd of guests attending the John P. Kee Concert

*Ira Combs III graduation from Ave Marie School of Law,
Naples, Florida*

*Sarah M. Combs graduation from
Eastern Michigan University*

Charles Anderson (first African American warden in the history of the state of Michigan), Bishop Ira Combs, Jr., and the legendary coach Tony Dungy (first African American NFL coach to win a Super Bowl) at an event at Greater Bible Way Temple

*Photo of the original church building of
Greater Bible Way Temple.*

Greater Bible Way Temple (GBWT) of Jackson, Michigan

Young Combs family at Cascade Manor House

Senator Dick Armey, Bishop Ira Combs, Jr.,
and Congressman Nick Smith

Senator Philip E. Hoffman and Bishop Ira Combs,
Jr., Senate Prayer

Ira Combs, Sr.

TRIBUTE IN MEMORY OF
MY FATHER: IRA COMBS, SR.

He was born into this world on March 22, 1927, to William Otis Combs and Anna Lee Reddick. A native of Michigan and the city of Detroit, Ira, Sr., was one of five children: one sister, Ann Lee Reddick; and three brothers, Wilbur Brown, Percy Brown, and Otis Combs, all who preceded him in departing this life.

He was baptized in the name of the Lord Jesus Christ and filled with the gift of the Holy Spirit under the ministry of the late Pastor Horace Jackson, Sr., in Romulus, Michigan. It was through this encounter with the gospel of Jesus Christ that his immediate family came in contact with the truth. Subsequent to him receiving the new birth experience, his wife Hazel Cummings was likewise baptized in the name of Christ Jesus, received the Holy Spirit, and has testified on occasion of one of the most extraordinary supernatural experiences in Christian history, which unfortunately is not a part of this record. Ira Combs, Sr., excelled in business and personal achievement, founding Combs Landscaping Services and Combs Plumbing and Heating with his older brother Otis Combs. Eventually he returned to academia to pursue an engineering degree as a high–pressure boiler operator. To his credit, he succeeded and was employed by Ford Motor Company in River Rouge, Michigan, in supervision, retiring in 1991 with thirty years of service.

After his retirement, his health began to fail and he was cared for by his precious daughter, Jacqueline Susan Combs-Lauwerys as well as a loving cousin, Melinda Minor. It can be concluded that as a result of the kindness and sacrifice of these two persons, he experienced an extension of life that otherwise would have evaded him. After the death of his daughter Jacqueline's husband Pierre, he was transitioned to be cared for by Kimberly Loretta Marshall Combs in Jackson, Michigan. There he moved into his own newly renovated apartment and received supports from Edwina Gibson and Dominica Gibson. It is unequivocal that the quality of care provided him by the untiring efforts of these dedicated ladies made his condition bearable in the climax of his life. Finally, he was referred by his primary care physician to twenty-four–hour nursing care. It was at this time he was transitioned to the Napoleon Road Residential Care Home. The staff in collaboration with Kimberly and Edwina provided exceptional care until he departed this life on the evening of June 26, 2004.

TRIBUTE IN MEMORY OF MY MOTHER: HAZEL M. COSPER

Hazel Marie Cummings was born into this world January 21, 1930, to Henry Otis Cummings and Daisy Hatney in the city of Atlanta, Georgia. As a young girl, she dreamed of an education and a professional career as a CPA. She excelled in the segregated public schools of the south until moving to the north at an early age with her mother, Daisy Hatney. Her mother moved to the city of Detroit after circumstances beyond her control and remarried R.C. Daniels. At the age of eighteen years old Hazel met and fell in love with Ira Combs, Sr. After a brief courtship, they married at the Oak Grove AME Church, 20055 Indiana Avenue, Detroit, Michigan, the Right Reverend A. Schley, Pastor of Oak Grove AME, presiding. From there they moved to Westland, Michigan to 28975 Powers Street in Nankin Township. To their marriage were born ten healthy children, seven girls and three boys.

The Combs' home was a traditional home with Ira Combs, Sr., working while Hazel Marie bore children and guided the home. While living in Westland, Ira and Hazel began to attend church services in Romulus, Michigan, at Bethany Apostolic Faith Church, where the late Elder Horace Jackson, Sr., was pastoring. It was here they came in contact with the full gospel of Jesus Christ, hearing, believing and obeying the command of God, being baptized in the name of the Lord Jesus Christ and filled with the gift of the Holy Spirit.

The personal testimonial of Hazel Marie is that she initially did not believe in the experience of speaking with other tongues as the Spirit of God gave utterance. However, after being filled and having the experience, she advised her pastor, Horace Jackson, Sr., whose reply was for her to pray that God would open her understanding. She subsequently sought God in prayer and shortly thereafter had a dream in which she was set in an Armenian camp in the Middle East bordering Iran and there among the residents of the camp began to speak to the people she encountered in their language of which she had no prior knowledge. When she woke from the dream, she prayed for understanding, and within the same week an article appeared in the local newspaper regarding an Armenian priest who was being assigned to an Armenian congregation in Southfield, Michigan.

She decided to attempt to contact the priest in an effort to authenticate her "glossolalia experience" (speaking with tongues). She was first of all surprised when she called the parish where the priest was. When she spoke with him, she explained her reason for calling and requested his help in her attempt to understand her dream as it related to her supernatural experience of speaking with tongues upon receiving the baptism of the Holy Spirit. He listened attentively to her testimony and agreed to help if he was able. She said, "I am going to pray, and if I speak in a language you are familiar with, will you confirm?" His reply was, "I will." As she began to pray, the Holy Spirit moved and she spoke as the Spirit gave her utterance. The Armenian priest paused and said to her this is unusual and he had never experienced such a thing, but that she was speaking in one of the languages of the Armenian people and he interpreted the language in which she spoke. It was her testimony that this confirmed in her mind the reality of the baptism of the Holy Spirit being a legitimate religious experience. She further stated from this point forward in her life she never doubted God or the authenticity of the Pentecostal experience.

The home of the Combs family was one of extreme discipline. Hazel Marie was very serious about her children's Christian behavior in the home and the community. All were required to attend school on time and perform academically at the head of their class. Achievement and scholarship were hallmarks of the Combs home. Discipline was enforced, some may say to a fault. However, the measurable outcomes in the children's performance support the position of Hazel Marie. All of her children graduated from high school, and all have obtained postgraduate degrees from bachelor's to PhDs. None have ever been in jail for more than a few hours, and for nothing more than a traffic violation unless there have been some recent developments since this obituary was penned.

Late in life both Hazel and Ira returned to school to finish their own personal, professional degrees: Ira Combs, Sr., in engineering as a high–pressure boiler operator where he served at the Ford River Rouge Plant as chief engineer until his retirement and Hazel Marie as an LPN, cosmetologist, and registered nurse at Grace Sinai Hospital in Detroit, Michigan. Hazel Marie later remarried Lee Cosper, Jr., on April 29, 1988, in a private ceremony presided over by the Reverend Eugene Rhodes in Detroit, Michigan. Lee was an extraordinarily accommodating husband who proved to be a loving, caring companion who preceded her in death.

Hazel Marie was well rewarded as Psalm 127:3 states, "Lo, children are an heritage of the LORD: and the fruit of the womb is his reward." Her geriatric years were filled with quality, excellent care. Her daughters visited her regularly. First Lady Kimberly Combs (daughter-in-law) provided personal care for her from 2012 until the date of her failed health in December 2017. Gifty Nona Paintsil was her live–in caregiver in her luxury condominium upon her return from Arbor Manor Nursing Home, where she received excellent therapy and skilled nursing services. Many thanks to Lloyd and Judy Canton for their quality care and kind supports. It was these amazing accommodations that made the sunset of her life one of joy and peace.

Hazel Marie leaves to cherish her memories ten children: Janice Iris (Nathan) Spencer, MBA; Ivy Maria (Sidney) Nickolas, BA; Teresa Dasia (Bernard) Richardson, PhD; Anna Lee Leslie Estelle Combs Allen, PhD; Ira (Kimberly) Combs, Jr., DD; Jacqueline Susan Lauwerys, MBA; LaDonna L. (Charles) Christian, PhD; William Miles (Marilou) Combs, RN, Ret. USAF EMT; Carla Anita Myshaun (Edward) O'Connell, BA; and Carlton Joseph Lamont Combs, BA; Twenty-five grandchildren: Nathan Jr., Stephan, Tabitha, Nelson, Jr., Nicholas, Joanna, Everett, Vincent, Justin, Marcus, Cassandra, Sarah, Ira III, Elisha, Ira Andrew, Jonathan, Isaiah, Micah,

Aaron, Carlton, Ethan, Kevin, Joshua, Brandon, Kirsten; twenty-seven great-grandchildren; and cousins John Hatney of Augusta, Georgia; Juanita Lazenby of Maywood, Illinois; and Cora Dodson of Atlanta, Georgia.

And now, Hazel Marie, sleep on, we will carry on and we shall see you in that great getting up morning, the Rapture of the Church. Glory!

ABOUT THE AUTHOR

BISHOP IRA COMBS, JR., DD.

Profile

Synopsis

Bishop Combs, DD, is a licensed and ordained minister carrying the title bishop with the Pentecostal Assemblies of the World, Inc., (PAW), the oldest and second–largest Pentecostal organization in the world. He is the founder and pastor of the Greater Bible Way Temple Church of the Apostolic Faith; the founder and executive director of Christ Centered Homes, Inc.; and the president and chairman of IRCO Housing Development, Inc., all in Jackson, Michigan. He and his wife, Kimberly, have two children.

Bishop Combs' degrees in theology, his role as a pastor, and his experience as an executive trained in finance present a rare combination of qualifications that enable him to lead with insight, compassion, and business savvy. An exceptional Bible teacher, community leader, and entrepreneur, Bishop Combs has received many awards and accolades.

Early Life

Bishop Combs was born in Ypsilanti, Michigan, at Beyer Memorial Hospital, to the late Ira Combs, Sr., and Hazel Combs in 1958. He was the fifth of ten children, raised in the city of Westland, Michigan. There, he attended Inkster Public Schools until matriculating to East Lansing High School in 1974–75. He graduated from East Lansing High School in 1976 as a college prep graduate and matriculated to Michigan State University, where he majored in business marketing and minored in religion from 1976–1979. During his tenure as a student at MSU, he was exposed to the megachurch ministry of Bishop David L. Ellis at Greater Grace Temple, Detroit, Michigan. On May 14, 1978, he accepted the new birth experience at Greater Grace Temple of being born again of water and spirit (John 3:5). It was this experience that led to his call to the ministry.

While continuing his academic pursuits at MSU, he was involved in many extra-curricular activities:

- He was recruited and became a member of Omega Psi Phi Fraternity, Sigma Chapter

- He was afterward recruited by the National Pan-Hellenic Council (NPHC) of MSU to serve as the president of its MSU campus chapter (by Andre DuPerry, director of procurements under Dave Bing)
- As president of the National Pan-Hellenic Council, he led and secured the effort for major governing body status for NPHC through campus legislative efforts of a university–wide vote
- He served as president of the NPHC on MSU President Clifton Wharton's committee to raise $17 million for the Clifton and Dolores Wharton Center for Performing Arts

Bishop Combs acknowledged the call of God on his life in May of 1978. He transferred all of his academic studies to Aenon Bible College and Indiana Bible College, Indianapolis, Indiana, to prepare for the pastorate in Jackson, Michigan.

During this time, the Northern District Council leadership, comprised of Bishop Ross P. Paddock (Diocesan of Fifth Episcopal Diocese), Elder William Warren, District Elder Harry L. Herman, and District Elder David L. Ellis, agreed to supervise the pioneering of the Greater Bible Way Temple Church of Jackson, Michigan, under their careful oversight. On November 25, 1980, Elder Combs established and incorporated the Greater Bible Way Temple of the Apostolic Faith at 327 W. Monroe Street, Jackson, Michigan. Earlier that year, he married Kimberly Marshall of Detroit. To this union was born their daughter, Sarah Michelle, and son, Ira III. Sarah Michelle is a graduate of Eastern Michigan University (Ypsilanti, Michigan) with a bachelor's degree in human resources. Ira III is a graduate of Ave Maria School of Law (Naples, Florida) with a juris doctorate in law.

Bishop Combs held career positions in Lansing at American Bank and Trust/PNC Bank from 1978–1980, Xerox Corporation from 1980–1986, and Primerica Insurance Company 1985–1986, serving as district manager in his Michigan region.

Ministerial and Educational Milestones

The next several years represented a season of growth and development for the pastoral ministry and the ongoing formal education of Bishop Combs.

- In 1989, he founded Christ Centered Homes, Inc. (CCH), a nonprofit organization that provides community staffing and housing as well as personal care services for the developmentally disabled. His decision to launch and manage CCH stems from his conviction that people of faith should care for the less fortunate. In his role as executive director, he uses his expertise in ministry, building projects, community outreach, and housing acquisition to manage the administration, develop the strategic plans, and oversee the nonprofit's values and missions.

- He has added to his credentials in this area of professionalism:
  Life member of the American Psychotherapy Association (APA) as of March 2008
  Member of the American College of Forensic Examiners Institute (ACFEI), March 2008

> Academy–certified master chaplain level III,
> APA, March 2008
> Certified in Homeland Security Level I, ACFEI,
> May 2008
> Certified master chaplain, CMC; American
> Board for Certification in Homeland
> Security (ABCHS), August 2010
> Awarded life diplomate status with the APA,
> December 2014
> Appointed to the board of directors, ABCHS,
> December 2015
> Awarded board–certified PTSD Counselor
> designation, February 2017

He also led his church through various phases of growth and development, from its original 400–square–foot building seating thirty to its current 42,000 square–foot building seating 1,200 at 322 Madison St., Jackson.

From 1998–2001, Bishop Combs served as vice chairman of the Pentecostal Assemblies of the World, Inc. (PAW), Northern District Council, overseeing 120 churches throughout Michigan and Canada. In 2010, he was elevated to the office of bishop and assigned as a member of the PAW Board of Bishops to the Forty-seventh Diocese, the country of Kenya, Africa, for the purpose of sustaining and establishing new churches throughout the country. He was successful in raising $100,000 in funds for foreign mission projects in Kenya from 2010–2014. In March 2014, he was appointed by the PAW Board of Bishops to the office of diocesan bishop, Fifth Episcopal District (Michigan/Canada).

Continuing Education and Preparation for Future Growth

Bishop Combs has pursued theological studies at several Christian institutions:

- Bachelor of Theology from Indiana Bible College, Indianapolis, Indiana, in 1991
- Master of Arts in Pastoral Ministry from Aenon Bible College, Indianapolis, Indiana, in 2013–14 for his published work, "17 Titles of a Pastor"
- Honorary Doctorate in 1999 from Aenon Bible College for his published work, "The Era of Apostolic Excellence – A Chronology of the Teachings of Bishop R.P. Paddock"
- Honorary Doctorate of Divinity in 2003 from Aenon Bible College
- Honorary Doctorate of Theology/Divinity from St. Thomas Christian College, Jacksonville, Florida, in 2006 for the successful expansion of the ministry in Jackson, Michigan
- Honorary Doctorate from Grace Bible College, Louisville, Kentucky, in 2006 for the successful completion of the new Greater Bible Way Temple Cathedral in Jackson, Michigan

Bishop Combs also studied finance at Oxford University, Oxford, England, as a member of the prestigious Oxford Club in 1995, of which he was a member for approximately twenty years.

Health, Housing, and Protection of Vulnerable Adults

Bishop Combs has demonstrated leadership in health, housing, and protection of the vulnerable in many positions, including professional boards and committees. In the area of healthcare, he historically served on the Jackson-Hillsdale Community Mental Health's Committee to Develop Fee for Service Contracts under the leadership of Dr. Christina Thompson.

He is the founder and executive director of Christ Centered Homes, Inc., and contracts with several mental health organizations to provide residential care and community supports for persons with developmental disabilities, autism, and mental illness. He is a former chairman of the AFC Licensing Advisory Council, appointed by Governor Rick Snyder, and served for an unprecedented three terms. In connection with his work in human services, he has the academic certification of diplomate with the American Psychotherapy Association as well as the Academy of Certified Master Chaplains. Both organizations set policy for healthcare institutions throughout the country and the world. He is also a member of the International Association of Emergency Managers (IAEM) and participates in annual National Homeland Security Conferences.

From 2000–2008, former president George W. Bush appointed Bishop Combs to serve as the director of faith–based initiatives for the state of Michigan, in which capacity he hosted annual local faith–based conferences. Keynote speakers included former first lady Laura Bush; former ambassador to the United Nations Dr. Alan Keys; former US attorney Eastern District, Juris Doctorate Jeffrey Collins; billionaire extraordinaire Dick DeVos, Jr., Amway Corporation; motivational speaker Les Brown; former Michigan state senator Philip E. Hoffman; former Michigan state representative Mike Murphy; former Michigan state representative Mickey Mortimer; former Michigan congressman Nick Smith; former congressman Joe Schwartz; former president of Spring Arbor University Gayle Beebe, PhD; former vice president of Hope Network Jim Tuinstra; former three–term governor of Michigan John Engler; members of the Michigan Supreme Court; and former Jackson County circuit judges Chad Schmucker and Charles Nelson, to mention a few.

In 2004–2008, Bishop Combs was recruited by White House adviser John Dunigan and recommended to Lee Scott, chairman of Walmart, to serve as a spokesperson with former ambassador Andrew Young (United Nations) for Working Families for Walmart. Bishop Combs was assigned the responsibility of chief spokesperson in the media to assist Walmart's effort to expand its corporate footprint into underserved urban areas throughout the United States. Ambassador Young negotiated contracts with municipalities in seven cities for Walmart to successfully build/develop stores and create job opportunities for these underserved areas.

State and Local Human Service Boards

- Served on the State Child Abuse and Prevention Board, appointed by former Michigan governor John Engler, 1999–2004
- Served on the Board of Directors for Choices for Children and Great Lakes Educational Program (GLEP) from 1995–2005
- Served on the local board of directors of Presbyterian Villages Springbrook Meadows, a faith–based nonprofit organization providing senior housing throughout the country, 2010–2011

- Served two three–year terms on the Michigan Attorney Discipline Board, 2001–2007

The Future

An exceptional Bible teacher, author, community leader, and philanthropist, Bishop Combs has received many awards and accolades for his God–driven accomplishments. Bishop Combs continues to fulfill his call and mission to preach the gospel of Jesus Christ. His life is a reflection of the simple commandment of Jesus Christ to "Follow me." He is inspired by the famous quote of Dr. Martin Luther King that states, in part:

"Everybody can be great, because anybody can serve. You don't have to have a college degree to serve. You don't have to make your subject and verb agree to serve . . . You only need a heart full of grace. A soul generated by love."

BIOGRAPHICAL HIGHLIGHTS

BORN
Ira Combs, Jr.
March 21, 1958
Ypsilanti, Michigan

PARENTS
The late Ira Combs, Sr., and Hazel Combs

MARRIED
Kimberly Marshall of Detroit, Michigan 1980

RESIDENCE
Jackson, Michigan

EMPLOYMENT
- Founder and pastor of Greater Bible Way Temple Church of the Apostolic Faith, 322 Madison Street, Jackson, Michigan
- Founder and Executive Director of Christ Centered Homes, Inc., 327 W. Monroe Street, Jackson, Michigan; a provider of residential services
- President and Chairman of IRCO Housing Development, Inc., 322 Madison Street, Jackson, Michigan

EDUCATION

- 2014 - Master of Arts in Pastoral Ministry, Aenon Bible College, Indianapolis, Ind.; published work: "17 Titles of a Pastor"
- 2006 - Honorary Doctorate of Theology and Divinity, St. Thomas Christian College, Jacksonville, Florida, and Grace Bible College, Louisville, Kentucky
- 2003 - Honorary Doctorate of Divinity, Aenon Bible College
- 1999 - Honorary Doctorate, Aenon Bible College; published work titled "The Era of Apostolic Excellence – A Chronology of the Teachings of Bishop R.P. Paddock"
- 1995 - Studied finance at Oxford University in Oxford, England
- 1991 - Bachelor of Theology, Indiana Bible College, Indianapolis, Indiana
- 1976-1979 - Studied business marketing at Michigan State University, Lansing, Michigan

HONORS and ACTIVITIES

- Served as a representative of the National Working Families for Walmart along with former ambassador Andrew Young and as a regular commentator on CNBC television for the retailer; made regular appearances in December 2005 and January 2006 on CNBC's "On the Money" segments with business day anchor, Dylan Ratigan, and Melissa Francis

- Featured on the cover and as lead story in the May 2000 and 2011 issues of *Jackson Magazine*
- Profiled in the 1997–98 American cirectory of *Who's Who in Executive and Business* and the 1994 international *Who's Who of Professionals in America*
- Profiled in the 1992–93 Marquis *Who's Who in Religion* and the 1990, 1992–93 Marquis *Who's Who in the Midwest*
- Received the YMCA Manny Fields Community Service Award in 1995; elected in 1982 by the National Jaycees as "Outstanding Young Man of America"
- Received Michigan State University National Pan-Hellenic "Outstanding Chairman" gavel award in 1977–79

ACADEMIC LEADERSHIP

- Founder and president of the National Pan-Hellenic Council while at Michigan State University (MSU), Lansing, Michigan, 1976–79
- Active member of the Omega Psi Phi Fraternity, Sigma Chapter; the ASMSU Policy Committee; the Student Media Appropriation Board; and a member of a $17,000,000 fundraising committee for the Delores Wharton Performing Arts Center, all while at MSU, 1976–79
- Served as a Student Advisory Group representative for the National Pan-Hellenic Council under the Edgar L. Hardin Administration (MSU President), 1976–79

ECCLESIASTICAL LEADERSHIP

- Licensed and ordained minister in 1981, carrying the title bishop with the Pentecostal Assemblies of the World (PAW), the oldest and second–largest Pentecostal organization in the world
- Elevated to the office of bishop in August 2010; assigned to the Forty-seventh Diocese, country of Kenya; served as a member of the Northern District Council Bishops Advisory Board
- Appointed by the Pentecostal Assemblies of the World in March 2014 to the office of Diocesan Bishop, Fifth Episcopal District overseeing 120 churches in Michigan/Canada
- Current member, board of directors Aenon Bible College, Indianapolis, Indiana; first vice president
- Served as vice chairman of the PAW Northern District Council, 1998–2001
- Writer for the PAW *Christian Outlook* magazine, the official publication of the organization
- Ministerial counselor for the Jackson County Sheriff's Department, Jackson, Michigan, 1995–present
- Former advisory board member for the Christian Action Network in St. Louis, Missouri (National Advisory Committee), 1990–1993

COMMUNITY SERVICE

- Current member of the Gerald R. Ford Presidential Foundation, Grand Rapids, Michigan, recruited by Steve Ford

- Former member board of directors for Choices for Children, founded by Betsy and Dick DeVos and Great Lakes Educational Program (GLEP), 1995–2005
- Former chairman Community Service Committee of the Jackson Rotary Club/Rotary Foundation
- Served as co-sponsor with Congressman Nick Smith on President Bush's faith–based initiative in Michigan and hosted annual Michigan Faith–Based Summits, 2000–2008
- Served on the advisory board of Starr Commonwealth, Albion, Michigan, 2002–2004
- Former member of the board of directors of the Jackson Chamber of Commerce
- Served as chairman of the Jackson, Michigan, chapter NAACP Freedom Fund Banquet Committee, which raised $22,000 in contributions in less than six months (under State Chair Carl Breeding)
- Served as Jackson City Police Reserve officer in 1996 and now serves as the Jackson City Police and County Sheriff chaplain

PROFESSIONAL ASSOCIATIONS and LEADERSHIP

- American 1 Credit Union board of directors ($120+ million credit union/tri-county area), August 2016–May 2018
- Appointed to the Spring Arbor University Board of Trustees, Jackson, Michigan, May 2016

- Reappointed to a third term and chairman (January 1, 2018–December 31, 2021) Michigan Department of Human Services Adult Foster Care Licensing Advisory Council
- Member of the Michigan Civil Rights Commission, February 1, 2018–December 2021
- Member of the International Association of Emergency Managers (IAEM), June 2018
- Awarded board–certified PTSD counselor designation, February 2017
- Appointed to the board of directors of the American Board for Certification in Homeland Security (ABCHS), December 2015
- Awarded life diplomate status with the American Board for Certification in Homeland Security, December 2014
- Life member of the American Psychotherapy Association and academy–certified master chaplain, ACMC-III, designation by the APA, March 2008
- Served on the Presbyterian Villages Springbrook Meadows board of directors, 2010–2011
- Served two terms as a member of the State Child Abuse and Neglect Prevention Board by former Michigan governor John Engler, 1999–2004
- Appointed by the Michigan Supreme Court and served two three–year terms on the Michigan Attorney Discipline Board that included such distinguished members as the Honorable Richard Suhrheinrich, the Honorable Wallace D. Riley,

and the Honorable William J. Danhof, 2001–2007
- Appointed by former Jackson mayor Betty Granger to serve as human relations commissioner on the Jackson City Human Relations Commission (Ex Officio), 1995
- First local chairman appointee of the Michigan Leadership Conference (Detroit) by state president and founder Joseph E. Madison, 1990
- Formerly served on the Jackson-Hillsdale Community Mental Health's Committee to Develop Fee for Service Contracts, as chairman of the Jackson-Hillsdale Community Mental Health Problem Solving and Solution Committee

POLITICAL ASSOCIATIONS and LEADERSHIP

- A ranking member of Governor Rick Snyder's re-elections teams for southeastern Michigan and Seventh District
- Served as vice chair of outreach for the Michigan Republican Party, state delegate for the Michigan Republican Party and co-chair of the Jackson Area Committee to Re-elect George W. Bush, and former chairman of the Recruitment Committee of the Jackson Republican Party
- Served on the National Exploratory Presidential Committee under the auspices of Michigan governor John Engler
- Became a Michigan team leader for the presidential campaign of President George W. Bush

- Appointed by the Honorable Congressman J.C. Watts to serve as a steering committee member of President George W. Bush's faith–based initiative
- Nominated by Congressman Nick Smith to be the Michigan representative for President George W. Bush's faith–based initiative
- Member of Governor John Engler's clergy commission and Senator Philip Hoffman's cabinet club, Congressman Nick Smith's cabinet club, and the executive committee of the Jackson Republican Party
- Received the Republican National Committee (RNC) Entrepreneur of the Year award in 2000 and was appointed to the RNC as representative of African American issues in 2004

BLESSINGS

*Beloved, I wish above all things that thou mayest prosper and
be in health, even as thy soul prospereth.*
(3 John 1:2)

I would like to recognize and bestow blessings on the following individuals who have contributed to the greater good of the community:

<u>Ecclesiastical Leadership</u>:
- Members of the board of bishops, Pentecostal Assemblies of the World
- Former bishops of the Northern District Council (Bishop David L. Ellis, DD; Bishop Willie L. Burrel, Sr., DD; Bishop Ross P. Paddock, D.D., Bishop Harry L. Herman, DD)
- Special tribute to Samuel Nathan Hancock, founder of the Northern District Council

Greater Bible Way Temple of Jackson, Michigan

Associate Pastors
Eric Beda, MBA
Gregory Crump, MBA
Maurice Fitzpatrick

Dennis Treadway
Geter Jenkins

Associate Ministers
Kimberly Crump, BS
Sauncha Brooks
Amber Wright
Eian Wright
Betty Briston

Technology
Calvin and Alicia Williams

Hospitality
Bertha M. Cotton

Greater Bible Way Temple Executive Board and Administration
Lucinda Treadway, MBA, Administrator
Stephen Nabors, MA, General Secretary
Associate Pastor Gregory Crump, MBA, Director

Administrative Assistants
Min. Kimberly Crump, BS
Ella Fitzpatrick
Coriena Haynes

Trustees
Maurice Amos,
Jeffery Briston

Samuel Frye
Edward Marshall
Stephen Nabors, MA
Lamar Selby
Lavoski Baker

Former associate pastors that are now bishops
Bishop Timothy O. Johnson, Sr., DD (Greater
Bibleway Temple, Montgomery, Alabama;
Diocesan, Sixth Episcopal District, Apostolic
Faith Fellowship International, Inc.)

Bishop Rader Johnson, PhD (Greater Bethel
Temple of the Apostolic Faith, Louisville,
Kentucky; Diocesan, Fifty-fourth Episcopal
District, Dominican Republic, Pentecostal
Assemblies of the World)

Chaplain's Program, Fidelis SeniorCare
Sam Willcoxon (former CEO/Fidelis
SeniorCare)
Jerry Wilborn, MD; former professor University
of Michigan (Thank you!)
Tom Selznick, DO
Adam Kelser, DO
District Elder Eunice Jones, chaplain's program
Robert Allen, MA, chaplain's program
coordinator
Elder Michael Shaw

International Diplomats

Ambassador Andrew Young (United Nations)
Ambassador Alan Keyes (United Nations)
Ambassador Ron Weiser (Slovakia)
Ambassador David P. Rawson (deceased)
(Rwanda and Mali)
Ambassador Joe J. Cella, Director of the Catholic
Vote Conference (Fiji Islands)

Politicians and Elected Officials

President George W. Bush
President Barack H. Obama
US Senator Debbie Stabenow (Michigan)
Governor John M. Engler, State of Michigan
Governor Rick D. Snyder, State of Michigan
Governor Gretchen E. Whitmer, State of
Michigan
Congressman Nick H. Smith, Seventh District
(nominated Bishop Ira Combs, Jr., to head
faith–based initiatives under President George
W. Bush)
Congressman John J. H. (Joe) Schwarz, M.D.,
Seventh District (CIA Attaché)
Congressman Timothy L. Walberg, Seventh
District
Congressman Mark H. Schauer, Seventh District
Congressman Mike D. Bishop, Eighth District/
Thirteenth senate majority leader
Congressman Mike J. Rogers, Eighth District
(chairman of Select Committee on Intelligence)

Congressman John J. Conyers, Jr., (D-Detroit,
Michigan)
Congressman Julius Caesar Watts, chairman of
House Republican Conference
State Senator David S. Holmes, Jr., Fourth
District
State Senator Mike Nofs, Nineteenth District
State Senator Philip E. Hoffman, Nineteenth
District
State Senator Cameron S. Brown, Sixteenth
District
State Senator Patrick Colbeck, Seventh District
Senate Majority Leader Ken R. Sikkema, Twelfth
District
Senate Majority Leader Randy Richardville,
Seventeenth District
Lieutenant Governor Dick Posthumus
(Governor John M. Engler)
Lieutenant Governor Brian N. Calley (Governor
Rick P. Snyder)
Lieutenant Governor Garlin Gilchrist II
(Governor Gretchen E. Whitmer)
Lieutenant Governor Jennifer Carroll (Governor
Rick Scott, State of Florida)
State Representative Joe Young, Sr. (deceased),
house appropriations chair
State Representative Clyde E. LeTarte (deceased)
State Representative Micky Mortimer
State Representative Julie Alexander
State Representative Ronnie D. Peterson, Fifty-
fourth District

Public Servants:

Elroy P. Sailor, director of faith–based initiatives, Congressman J.C. Watts Companies

Angela Sailor, director of RNC, African American Outreach/Heritage Foundation

Lowell W. Perry (deceased), director of urban affairs (Governor John M. Engler)

James K. Haveman, director of HHS (Governor John M. Engler/Governor Rick Snyder)

Tom D. Watkins, Jr., former director of Michigan Department of Mental Health (Governor Jim Blanchard)

Saul Anuzis, former chairman, Michigan Republican Party

Dr. Christina Thompson, PhD, former director of LifeWays

Ed Woods, M.E., LifeWays board of directors chair, Mid-State Health Network

Harvey Hollins III, former director of Office of Urban Initiatives (Governor Rick Snyder)

Richard D. McLellan, Esq., founder of Michigan Economic Development Corporation and Mackinaw Center for Public Policy

Sandy Keener, RN (deceased), Lenawee CMH

Kathy A. Szewczuk, executive director, Lenawee CMH

Law Enforcement:

Hank C. Zavislak, former Jackson County sheriff/Jackson County prosecutor

Daniel Heyns, Jackson County sheriff/director,
Michigan Department of Corrections
Sheriff Steve Rand, Jackson County sheriff
Jackson County sheriff Gary R. Schuette
Chief Kent Maurer, Jackson City Police
Lieutenant David Zomer, Jackson City Police
Chief Ervin Portis, chief, Jackson City Police
Chief Matthew R. Heins, Jackson City Police
Chief Elmer Hitt, director, Jackson City Police
Sheriff Michael J. Bouchard, Oakland County
Sheriff/state senator
Tom J. Ridge, US secretary of Homeland Security
Colonel Kriste K. Etue, retired director of
Michigan State Police
Captain Troy Allen, commander, Michigan State
Police
Captain Emmit McGowan, Michigan State
Police
Detective Robert Pertuso, former FBI special
agent
Detective Wayne Bullen
Jeff Kirkpatrick, Judicial Services Group
Officer Ruben Soto, South Haven Police
Captain Scott Rogers, Jackson City Police
Chief Robert Johnson, first African American
Police Chief, City of Lansing, Michigan

Judges (Jackson County):
Judge John G. McBain, JD
Judge Thomas D. Wilson, JD

Judge Charles A. Nelson, JD (deceased)
Judge Edward J. Grant, JD (Thank you for
keeping the community safe!)
Judge Chad C. Schmucker, Chief Judge (retired)
Judge Carlene Lefere, JD (D)
Judge Diane Rappleye, JD
Judge Joseph S. Filip, JD
Prosecutor Jerry M. Jarzynka

Judges, Michigan Appeals Court

The Honorable Judge Jeffrey G. Collins, US
attorney, Eastern District/Michigan Supreme
Court
The Honorable Judge Curtis T. Wilder, US
Appeals Court/Michigan Supreme Court
The Honorable Judge Bill D. Schuette, US
Appeals Court/fifty-third Michigan attorney
general/Michigan Senate

Michigan Supreme Court

The Honorable Robert P. Young, Jr.
The Honorable Brian K. Zahra
The Honorable Maura D. Corrigan (retired)
The Honorable Steven J. Markman
The Honorable Cliff W. Taylor
The Honorable Conrad L. Mallett, Jr. (D)

Federal Court

The Honorable Richard F. Suhrheinrich, Sixth
Circuit Court of Appeals

Lawyers

Anne Lawter, Esq., Ringler and Associates

Sean F. Carroll, Esq., Sean F. Carroll PC

Anthony Raduazo, Esq. (retired), Brown Raduazo and Hilderly PLLC

Tony G. Arnone, Esq. (deceased) Kitch Drutchas Wagner Valitutti & Sherbrook

R. Vincent Green, attorney at law

Lynn McGuire Esq., Butzel Long, Ann Arbor, Michigan

Eric Doster, Esq., Doster Law Offices PLLC

Jay A. Sekulow, Esq., president of American Center for Law and Justice, Washington, DC

Richard Thompson, Esq., president and chief counsel, Thomas More Law Center, Ann Arbor Michigan

Michigan Attorney Discipline Board

Wallace D. Riley, Esq., former chairperson of Attorney Discipline Board

Theodore J. St. Antoine, Dean, University of Michigan Law School/former chairperson Attorney Discipline Board

William J. Danhof, former US attorney general/ former chairperson of Attorney Discipline Board

The Honorable Richard F. Suhrheinrich, Sixth Circuit Court of Appeals/Attorney Discipline Board

Education:

Richard D. McLellan, Esq. (author of charter school legislation)

Dick and Betsy DeVos (Choices for Children, Great Lake Education Program)

Clark Durant (Cornerstone Schools)

East Lansing High School college prep program

Dr. William Ealy (deceased), counselor, Inkster High School

Clifton R. Wharton, Jr., president, Michigan State University (Clifton and Dolores Wharton Performing Arts Center)

Edgar L. Harden, (deceased) former president, Michigan State University and former president of Story Oldsmobile

Jack Shingleton, Director of Student Services, Michigan State University

Dean Robert L. Green, PhD, dean of the College of Urban Development, Michigan State University

Earvin "Magic" Johnson, fellow student

Jay Vincent, fellow student

Kirk Gibson, fellow student

Members of the National Pan-Hellenic Council of African American Fraternities and Sororities (historic designation in the MSU Department of African American History)

1. Omega Psi Phi (F)
2. Kappa Alpha Psi (F)
3. Phi Beta Sigma (F)

4. Delta Sigma Theta (S)
5. Alpha Kappa Alpha (S)
6. Zeta Phi Beta (S)

Dr. Carl Taylor, PhD
Dr. Charles Roberts, PhD
Dr. Bernard Richardson, PhD (brother-in-law; dean of Howard Chapel, Howard University)
Dr. Brent D. Ellis, president, Spring Arbor University
Dr. Gayle D. Beebe, former president, Spring Arbor University

Civil Rights:

Joe Madison, syndicated radio talk–show host ("The Black Eagle")
Governor Rick D. Snyder (in appointing me to the Michigan Civil Rights Commission)
William F. Pickard, PhD, founder/chairman of Global Automotive Alliance (parts supplier to GM, Ford, and Chrysler)

Banking and Finance

Jim Dutmers, VP, American Bank and Trust
John Curry, VP, (deceased) American Bank and Trust
Bill Siegrist, VP, (deceased) American Bank and Trust
Jim Herrick, VP, (deceased) American Bank and Trust

Vick Loomis, assistant VP, American Bank and
Trust/president of MSU Credit Union
John Mansour, workout department, American
Bank and Trust
Kady Haar, (deceased) president of mortgage
department, American Bank and Trust
Clyde McKenzie, VP, American Bank and Trust
Frederick L. Davies, President, Comerica Bank-
Jackson (worked with Fair Banking Practices
Initiatives in the State of Michigan)
Tom Melton, senior VP, Comerica Bank-Lansing
John Hendricks, VP, Comerica Bank-Detroit
Bill Brooks, former Comerica Bank board
member
Chuck Maurer (deceased), Old Kent Bank/Fifth
Third Bank
John Paul, president, Fifth Third Bank-
Kalamazoo
Jeff Herrington, VP, Fifth Third Bank-Battle
Creek
Tim Doyle, VP, Fifth Third Bank-Grand Rapids
Richard DeVos, Jr., Principal, Fifth Third Bank
Bill Jors, VP business development, County
National Bank
John R. Waldron, former president and CEO,
County National Bank

Family

Immediate Combs Family: Kimberly, Sarah M.,
Ira III, and Autumn Allen

ENDNOTES

1   George W. Bush, *A Charge to Keep* (New York: Harper Collins, 2001), 213.

2   "Former Detroit Emergency Manager Kevyn Orr Joins Lincoln Institute of Land Policy Board," LILP, May 23, 2018, http://lincolninst.edu/pt-br/news/lincoln-house-blog/former-detroit-emergency-manager-kevyn-orr-joins-lincoln-institute-land.

3   Saagar Enjeti, "FLASHBACK: All The Times Past Presidents Promised To Move US Embassy To Jerusalem," *Daily Caller,* December 6, 2017, http://dailycaller.com/2017/12/06/flashback-all-the-times-past-presidents-promised-to-move-us-embassy-to-jerusalem/.

4   "Immigration," Trump White House, posted May 21, 2019, https://trumpwhitehouse.archives.gov/issues/immigration.

5   Kurt M. Campbell and Ely Ratner, "The China Reckoning: How Beijing Defied American Expectations," *Foreign Affairs,* March/April 2018, 60-70.

6   Campbell and Ratner, "The China Reckoning," 63.

7   Campbell and Ratner, "The China Reckoning," 64.

8   Graham Allison, "China vs. America: Managing the Next Clash of Civilizations," *Foreign Affairs,* September/October 2017, 81.

9   Harry G. Gelber, *Nations Out of Empires: European Nationalism and the Transformation of Asia* (New York: Springer, 2001).